3427 £10

I ♥ HANDMADE BOOKS

First published in 2014 by
Jacqui Small LLP
An imprint of Aurum Press
74-77 White Lion Street
London N1 9PF

Commissioning editor: Isheeta Mustafi
Editor: Ellie Wilson
Assistant editor: Tamsin Richardson
Art director: Lucy Smith
Cover design: Michelle Rowlandson
Book layout: Lucy Smith, Michelle Rowlandson and Rebecca Hawkins
Illustrations: Hannah Rhodes

Typeset in Bodoni and Hero

ISBN: 978 1 909342 65 1

A catalogue record for this book is available from the British Library.

2016, 2015, 2014
10 9 8 7 6 5 4 3 2 1

Printed in China by 1010

Image credits (opposite):
Left: Cassandra Fernandez.
Centre: Luisa Gomez Cardoso,
Cantiero de Alfaces.
Right: Hu Jin, H&G Handmade.

I ♥
HANDMADE BOOKS

Timeless Techniques and Fresh Ideas for Beautiful Handmade Books

jacqui
small

CHARLOTTE RIVERS

CONTENTS

FOREWORD

I am honoured that Charlotte asked me to write this foreword and included Purgatory Pie Press's limited editions in this little book.

Although I have been active in this community for decades, many of these contributors are new to me, which makes me wonder: could book craft be overtaking knitting and quilting? It's easier to start. You don't need much specialist equipment - just paper. But you can delve deep into book arts, exploring the intricacies of the craft, such as gilding, papermaking, fine printing and edge painting.

In different places people use different names for tools, techniques and bindings. My 'origami snake' book (invented by Anna Wolf) is the Western New York Book Arts Center's (WNYBAC) 'dragon' book. Some instructions differ from my methods, but work for some people - which reminds me of the story of re-binding my first book.

When I moved to New York City, besides going dancing and learning which Chinatown restaurants stayed open past 2am, I hung out at the Center for Book Arts (CBA), where my future collaborator Dikko Faust was the letterpress printer. I loved stitching and working with my hands as a costume designer and figured I could re-bind a book. I got a tattered 1940s sewing manual from a thrift store and took it to CBA, knowing they could help me.

Re-binding is a slow process. People came and went, and advised me as I worked. But each new person told me I was doing it wrong as I followed the last person's directions. It was frustrating, but I finished. My book was not perfect - I'd had trouble trimming my endsheets and one had stretched and wrinkled when I pasted it. But I had accomplished my task and learnt I'd rather design than repair books for a living. The most important thing I learnt was that everyone told me something different and everyone was right. There are many ways to do it.

Find inspiration in the works within this book and try the projects at the end. See if you prefer folding or stitching, or if (unlike me) you like to glue. If something doesn't work for you, invent your own way of doing it. Maybe I will see your books on Etsy next year, or even have the chance to include them in an exhibit that I curate.

Have fun, and (as I say when I inscribe *How to Make Books*) MAKE BOOKS NOT WAR!

Esther

Esther K Smith ~ Purgatory Pie Press

ABOUT THIS BOOK

Bookbinding is an open, multi-disciplinary craft, which can incorporate illustration, graphic design, photography, printing, needlework, papercraft and many other creative disciplines. This is one reason why it is so appealing to creatives, who can bring their particular set of talents and passions into the process of crafting a handmade book.

A centuries-old craft, contemporary book-makers are finding new ways to interpret traditional binding techniques to create beautiful artisan books. This book aims to showcase the diversity and craftsmanship involved, and inspire you to make your own.

The first section presents a showcase of the inspirational work of book-makers from all around the world. We begin by looking at methods of folded bindings, showing how a single sheet of paper can be transformed into pages for a book, or combined to create flowing origami structures. Then we focus on sewn bindings and the array of different stitches, both functional and decorative, employed to bind pages and covers together. Having looked at ways to physically assemble a book, we then move on to look at different creative treatments for pages and covers and experimental packaging. These inspirational profiles feature a 'See Also', helping you find more information about relevant techniques used.

The final section of this book provides practical step-by-step tutorials for re-creating some of the techniques featured throughout, beginning with different folds, then stitches, then page and cover treatments.

A resources section at the back provides useful links to help you delve deeper into the world of book arts. By the time you turn the final page, hopefully you will be inspired and equipped to translate your own unique set of skills into a handmade book.

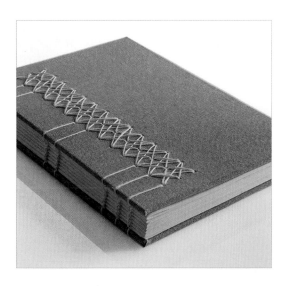

ANATOMY OF A BOOK

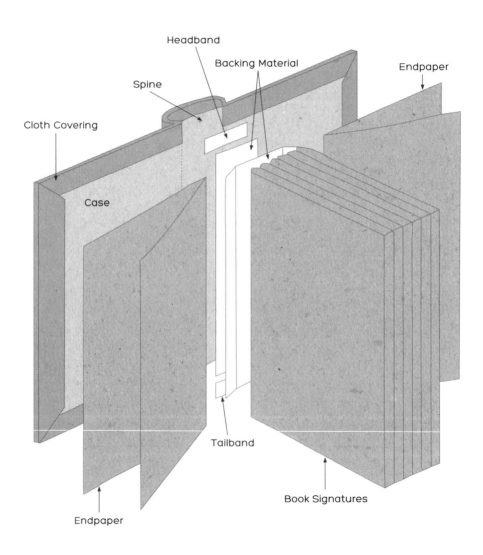

Headband

Backing Material

Spine

Endpaper

Cloth Covering

Case

Tailband

Endpaper

Book Signatures

Shown opposite is the anatomy of a typical case-bound book. Many of the artist books that you will find within the pages of this book employ this binding, but myriad different interpretations and experimentations of bookbinding techniques are also showcased. You will find folded books, sewn books, books with exposed spines, books with shell covers and books with wooden cases.

The descriptions of specific bookbinding terms can be found in the glossary on pages 188-9, but here are some key elements that make up the anatomy of a typical case-bound book.

Book Signatures

A signature is formed of a number of pages folded together. They are then sewn together to form a text block, or the inside pages of a book. Signatures in most commercial printed books are *octavos* (16 pages per signature), where a single sheet is folded in half three times.

Endpapers

Folded sheets of paper, known as endpapers, are pasted to the inside front cover and first page, and to the inside back cover and last page.

Headbands and Tailbands

These help secure the book, although they are not essential and are mainly used for decorative purposes. They can be hand-stitched.

Case

The case of a book is made using hard board covers and secures the book together.

Cloth Covering

Book cloth is often used to cover the book boards before they are made into a case.

Backing Material

Often made from mull, the backing material is applied to the spine of the book to help hold the pages in place and to secure the book to the cover.

Spine

The spine is the backbone of the book, holding all the signatures together.

1
FOLDED BINDINGS

Folded books offer some of the simplest, yet also the most innovative ways to turn a sheet (or sheets) of paper into a book. They require little else than the paper you are working with. Some cases will involve a little glue or thread, but essentially most require careful measuring, folding and scoring.

There are countless different ways to create folded books, and throughout this chapter we explore some interesting techniques, both traditional and more experimental. From Cassandra Fernandez's beautiful carousel-bound 'Kaleidobooks' to Becca Hirsbrunner's colourful lotus-fold and modified Turkish-fold books, and Christopher Skinner's carefully measured and scored single-sheet blizzard-fold book, each example should excite and inspire. In addition, they will demonstrate how different variations of materials and techniques can be used to create unique folded books.

CASSANDRA FERNANDEZ

BARCELONA, SPAIN

Hailing from Barcelona, Spain, artist Cassandra Fernandez primarily works with linocuts, making colourful prints and patterns. But, as can be seen here, she also likes to experiment with bookbinding techniques.

'I like to build things and make them by hand. I am a self-taught bookbinder, which I got into because I wanted to participate at an artist book fair taking place in Barcelona. What I like the most about the process of making an artist book is building the book itself and seeing if the idea I had in my mind really works.'

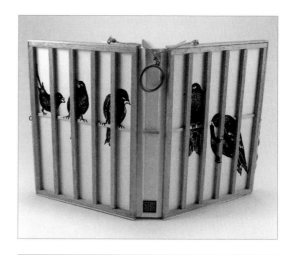

Fernandez's love of geometric patterns can be seen in her series of carousel 'Kaleidobooks' (opposite). The idea behind their creation was to make a book of patterns where one pattern merged into the next, creating a new pattern - a metamorphosis of patterns. Using the same carousel technique, Fernandez's book *Among Humans* (this page) simulates a birdcage when closed, but opens up completely into a carousel shape that can be hung by a string, using the attached ring, showing the birds flying free. Both books use Hahnemühle paper stock onto which Fernandez has hand-printed her beautiful linocut illustrations.

See also:
Carousel book page 140

KAROLIN SCHNOOR

LONDON, UK

Karolin Schnoor is an illustrator from Berlin who currently lives in South London, where she works on a variety of projects: designing books, pattern work, advertising, editorial and screenprinting.

'My main focus is illustration and I enjoy applying my drawings to three-dimensional objects, whether they are ceramics, textiles or small home-made books such as this one. I like seeing how an illustration changes when it's used in a more narrative context like a book.'

To create this small book - it measures 7 x 10cm (2³/₄ x 4in) - Schnoor first calculated how many pages she could fit on the sheets she was printing on, then measured out the exact format and where the page divisions were going to be. She then created the illustrations within these guidelines so the book would work when folded. The cover and insides were then screenprinted, cut and glued by hand. The cover was made using grey board and the inside pages have been printed on a newsprint stock.

See also:
Accordion book page 134

NAUGHTY DOG PRESS

IOWA CITY, IOWA, USA

Emily Martin creates limited-edition artist books and prints under the name of her studio, Naughty Dog Press. She uses a variety of print methods, including letterpress, and often experiments with three-dimensional forms for her books.

The Tragedy of Romeo and Juliet (above right) is a carousel book that uses a format Martin has devised, allowing for scenes to be in separate sections from the text, which sits on different panels.

Fly Away (below right) is a triangular accordion and a non-traditional variation of the Japanese double-leaved album, featuring a hard cover wrapped in Moriki paper. There are three texts that run along different facets of the book. When the book is standing upright all three facets are visible.

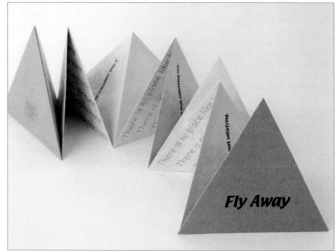

See also:
Accordion book page 134
Carousel book page 140

GABRIELA IRIGOYEN HANDMADE BOOKS

RIO DE JANEIRO, BRAZIL

For Rio-based book artist Gabriela Irigoyen, designing and making books is all about creating books that amaze people; books that are made as art. Working with all manner of materials, papers, threads and cloths, Irigoyen is continually researching new ways to create and construct her books.

'When it comes to making books, I love the research, thinking about how a book might look, and then, when the book is finished, seeing if the idea worked.'

These triangle accordion books were inspired by Irigoyen's desire to make a book using a shape other than the usual square or rectangle. She first created the inner pages of the books using an accordion fold format as inspiration.

Separately sewn triangular-shaped signatures were fixed together on the accordion-folded card. These were then fixed to board covers that had been bound in book cloth. Cord and ribbon are used to secure the books when they are closed.

See also:
Accordion book page 134

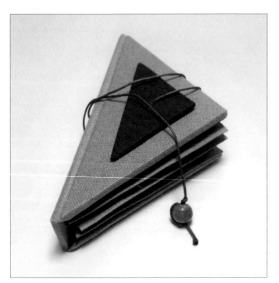

THEREZA ROWE

LONDON, UK

Thereza Rowe is a freelance illustrator and graphic designer. Colour and shape form the backbone of her work, which has a playful edge. She aims for her designs to bring a smile to the viewer's mind.

'I love making my own books and have a thing for fold-up ones. I especially like the process because it concerns problem-solving as well as free creative thinking. Seeing the finished artefact is, of course, a joy in itself, but the part that I treasure is the creating phase.'

Shown here are two of Rowe's folded books, *Tiny Neighbourhood* (this page and opposite, above) and *Portal Encantado* (opposite, below). *Tiny Neighbourhood* was created as a personal project exploring both Rowe's real and imaginary neighbourhoods. Made in a limited edition of 25,

it features the use of cut-outs and collages, which were edited in Adobe Photoshop and printed out in a line to give the idea of a street unfolding as the viewer opens the book.

Portal Encantado explores Brazilian folklore and tales. Rowe created a series of illustrations using pen, paper and collage, which again were edited in Photoshop. She has placed a window on the front cover of the book to convey the idea of a portal to an enchanted world. As the book unfolds, the viewer can peek through the window and see various scenes interacting within the book.

See also:
Accordion book page 134

ANNEKE DE CLERCK

JABBEKE, BELGIUM

Anneke De Clerck lives in a small village near the coast of Belgium, where she works as a midwife by day and a book artist by night.

'In my free time I'm always busy with my hands. I have a great passion for paper and stamps, and I love making cards, books and boxes. I'm also fond of recycling and like to make books with recycled materials, such as egg cartons, envelopes, used paper bags, all kinds of packaging materials, drinks cans and so on.'

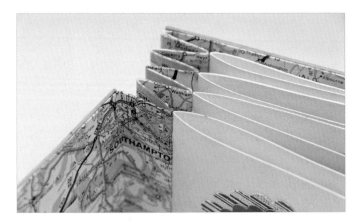

This book was created to document a family trip to Sussex, England. It is a pamphlet-sewn concertina binding. To create it De Clerck folded a strip of paper from a map of the UK to create an accordion fold - this is the basic approach for the concertina structure. She then attached inner pages to each peak of the spine using pamphlet stitch. A green-coloured handmade stock was used on the cover and a heavyweight cream stock was used for the inside pages.

See also:
Accordion book page 134
Pamphlet stitch page 146

KYLE HOLLAND

Kyle Holland is an interdisciplinary artist who creates artist books using various techniques, including letterpress printing, handmade paper and printmaking processes. Holland grew up making visual journals - altered books utilizing painting and collage elements. His initial exposure to bookbinding was through a Sculptural and Movable Books class with Emily Martin of Naughty Dog Press (see page 15) at Penland School of Crafts in North Carolina.

Holland was born and raised in Memphis, Tennessee, and his artist books respond to the culture of the South of the USA, primarily the Southern concept of masculinity.

Force of Circumstance is a flag book that represents the theme of hunting as a signifier of masculinity in Southern culture by fragmenting an image of a deer.

See also:
Flag book page 136

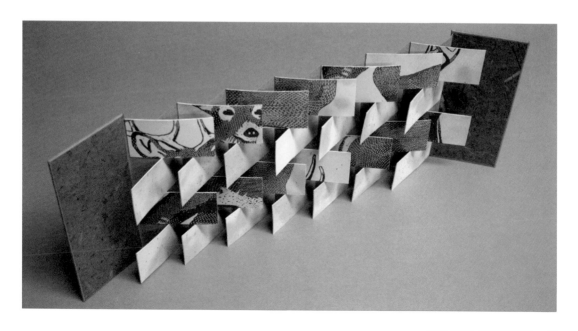

RUTH BLEAKLEY

COCOA BEACH, FLORIDA, USA

'I love the way that you can lose yourself in the repetitive motion of folding and stitching, over and over, and get into a very relaxed, but focused, state that I've heard called flow. Some people would describe it as tedious, but I half-jokingly refer to it as meditative.'

Ruth Bleakley is a Florida-based designer, book artist and teacher. She became interested in bookbinding by chance, but has now been creating books for more than five years.

Shown here are her miniature accordion books. Created using a simple accordion format, the covers are made of board and different types of patterned washi tape. 'I love the patterns and textures of the washi tapes and thought it would be fun to combine the tapes in different ways to make the covers of these tiny books. The adhesive on the tape meant that putting together these little books was even faster, because I didn't have to glue the covers on.'

See also:
Accordion book page 134

BECCA HIRSBRUNNER

Becca Hirsbrunner works as a type designer for SIL International. In her own time she likes to explore other artistic avenues, from bookbinding to hand-lettering to stained-glass mosaics.

Hirsbrunner tends to specialize in sewn bindings (see page 67) but she also experiments with folded books. The colourful lotus book (below) was made using a number of folded pages glued together, which, when opened, fan out like a flower opening. Hirsbrunner used origami paper for the pages and Italian cloth-bound book board for the cover.

An Echo Thrown (opposite) includes a modified version of the Turkish fold. Created out of a square piece of paper, the technique features three main folds: two along the diagonals, and then once in half. A triangle is formed by tucking in the opposite sides along the horizontal fold. This is known as a 'waterbomb' origami fold, minus the second

horizontal fold. Each of the four corners of the triangle is then folded towards the centre, unfolded and inverted so they can be tucked inside the main triangle. The edges resemble an accordion.

Hirsbrunner used Turkish fold for the inner four pages, but cut away part of the sides so the inner section of the fold would be revealed, even while closed. 'I used a two-section sewing technique to sew two of the pages together, twice for each side. I then glued the inside surface between the two pages together, and then the covers to the outer surface of the pages. Finally, I created another smaller Turkish fold out of white art paper, cut it in half, and glued it to the front and back covers alongside the larger folds.'

See also:
Dragon book page 138

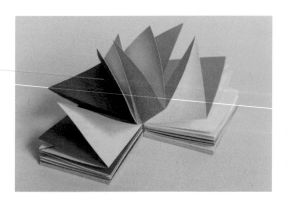
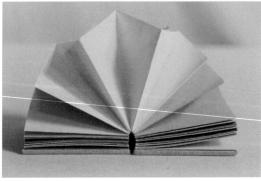

HILARY LECKRIDGE

'I wanted to make a book where the form echoed the content. This seven-pointed star-shaped book has the astrological constellations of the zodiac scattered over its pages. The inspiration for it came from an idea I heard expressed by an astronomer - that 'we are all made of starstuff'.

In her studio in central Scotland, Hilary Leckridge crafts individual and unusual artist books. Her love of book-making has grown out of a passion for handmade paper - in particular, washi paper, selected and brought back from trips to Japan.

This book, *Ecliptic*, is a modified crown binding inspired by stars. To create the book, Leckridge first folded the pages in four and punched small holes in the middle two sections to form the design of the constellations. The 'stars' were then joined by simple embossed lines to show the connections between them. The raw edges of the pages have been joined together using Japanese tissue, and this fold was then slotted into the spine of the crown binding. As a final touch, small electric lights can be inserted into the star sections when the book is upright so that the stars shine in the dark.

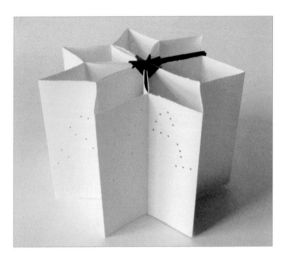

RED PARROT PRESS

EL CERRITO, CALIFORNIA, USA

Red Parrot Press is run by printmaker and book artist Barbara Milman, who is based in the San Francisco Bay Area. Milman makes original handmade books using hand-pulled and digital prints, often in the folded accordion format.

The book shown here, *Marin Headlands 2010-2050*, was created as part of a series about climate change. It features Milman's images of the Marin Headlands, an area just north of San Francisco. She has assembled it as a two-sided accordion that can be read from either side. One side features images of the headlands as they are today; the other shows the same images, only they have been altered to reflect what Milman believes is likely to happen to the headlands as a result of climate change.

Milman chose the accordion format because it allows for a continuous design from page to page, and, in this book, permitted the double-sided approach, which was integral to the design and purpose of the book. She used Premier Smooth Fine Art paper for the book, which was then mounted on archival illustration board. The book was secured using linen tape.

See also:
Accordion book page 134

SAKURASNOW

AMSTERDAM, THE NETHERLANDS

Suzanne Norris is the graphic designer, illustrator and artist behind sakurasnow. Like many graphic designers, she works mainly on the computer, so likes to spend as much time as possible using her hands; creating illustrations in pen and ink, screenprinting, papercutting and sometimes making books, such as notebooks and sketchbooks.

This accordion book, entitled *13 Wonders from a Cabinet of Curiosities*, was created as part of a collaborative exhibition held in Jersey City and Brooklyn, New York. 'I had been working on an ongoing series of brush, pen and ink drawings of creatures in jars, loosely titled 'Wonders from a Cabinet of Curiosities', which I then translated into small, limited-edition screenprints. For the exhibition I chose to gather 13 of these creatures

together, creating a tangible object that could be perused like the *wunderkabinetts* of old. The accordion book form served this purpose very well.'

The scales on the cover were cut using Marpa Jansen 130gsm Grey Shadings Tinted papers and stuck to a sheet of heavyweight Schoellershammer tracing paper. This created a scaly 'skin', which was then affixed to the pocket cover card. The pocket cover and bellyband were made from dark blue Florentine 300gsm card, while the inner pages are light cream-coloured Simili Japon 225gsm stock.

See also:

Accordion book page 134

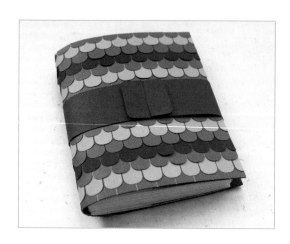

ELIZABETH SHEEHAN

Elizabeth Sheehan is a printmaker and papermaker with a background in sculpture. Creating artist books combines her interest in three-dimensional work with her love for handmade paper and printmaking.

Coruscation is an edition of five that began as a digital composition. Once Sheehan had finalized the design, she made photopolymer plates for the forms to be letterpress-printed, and films that she burned into screens for the forms that would be screenprinted. The digital layer was the first to be executed, followed by the screenprinting, letterpress printing and, finally, the addition of pop-ups.

See also:
Accordion book page 134

LITTLE PAPER BIRD

This treasure box of folded and sewn bound books was created by Leeds-based artist Sarah Peel of Little Paper Bird. 'I like making a lot of little books. Trying out new ideas, practising old ones, folding up strips of paper to see how they unfold again, adding a page here or there . . . Because I have so many I decided to make a cloth-covered box to keep them all in. I then wanted someone to open the box, be intrigued by the contents, take them out and be happily surprised by what they discover.'

Peel's box features a variety of folded bindings, including concertina, flexagon, accordion and other folds that Peel created herself. The books also feature some sewn bindings, including pamphlet stitch and Coptic stitch. 'I love the simplicity of pamphlet stitch. It's so versatile and functional, and concertina folding fascinates me; I wonder if I'll ever get bored of folding a piece of paper into a perfect little concertina.'

For the books, Peel used 160gsm cartridge stock, smooth Fabriano stock and light Tempura paper. The box was created using 3mm (⅛in) grey board and book cloth, and Mi-Teintes paper for the lining.

See also:
Accordion book page 134
Coptic stitch page 152
Pamphlet stitch page 146

CHRISTOPHER SKINNER

For designer, artist, bookbinder and printmaker Christopher Skinner, creating handmade books is all about working with whatever materials he has available. 'I am happy using commercially made papers and boards, and have also recently begun making my own papers from recycled junk mail and packaging. I prefer papers and boards with good textures, and enjoy mixing different papers within each project.'

The book shown here was created as part of Skinner's ongoing investigation into asemic writing, or writing with no semantic content.

The blizzard fold, made from a single sheet, involves careful measuring, folding and scoring. Skinner used a reasonably heavy 150gsm watercolour paper to allow the book to spring open naturally and create a neat fan structure. He chose to add separate cover boards and leave the spine exposed so that the book opened and lay flat.

'I like the overtly origami-like qualities of this technique and the fact that once folded it holds itself together; simple, but brilliant. Plus, it looks far more complicated than it is.'

LUCY MAY SCHOFIELD

Lucy May Schofield is an artist working primarily with paper and print. 'My practice attempts to capture moments, focusing on the overlooked. I consistently document vulnerability. I am fascinated by investigating the unspoken and record these moments in the form of paintings, prints, installations and artist books.'

Schofield works in various print forms, from letterpress, monoprinting, etching, silkscreen and risograph to photocopying and photography. She makes everything by hand, crafting both books and boxes. The series of 'Roadkill' books (right and opposite) were created using a single-sheet origami structure with cloth hardcovers, heat-foil-blocked in gold and silver foil with a copper die.

Letters of Triangles (below right) was inspired by the letters sent by Russian soldiers during World War II. These letters were folded into triangular forms, where the letter and envelope were one. This allowed censors to access and omit any sensitive material without compromising the structure. Schofield created this book about homesickness using found papers and tracing papers, letterpress-printed in copper and gold ink, which were folded into triangular shapes and overlaid on top of one another.

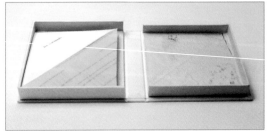

See also:
Dragon book page 138

FLYING FISH PRESS

BERKELEY, CALIFORNIA, USA

Julie Chen is the artist behind Flying Fish Press and has been publishing limited-edition books for more than 25 years. Shown here is her book *Cat's Cradle*. The intention behind its design was to translate thoughts about the nature of existence from idea to form, by employing the book structure itself as a visual and physical model of concepts portrayed in the text. To this end, it has been created using the carousel binding technique, which allows for the book to be viewed in two very distinct ways: circularly, with the cover boards drawn open 360 degrees so that they are touching, or linearly, when they are stretched apart like an accordion.

The pages were printed digitally and then laser-cut before being assembled. Chen has used cloth-covered book board for the covers, which are fastened closed with a ribbon. A magnetic hinge in the spine secures the book when opened 360 degrees. Chen aims for her book to provide a reading experience as well as to be displayed as a sculpture.

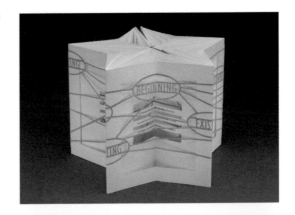

See also:
Carousel book page 140

BIG BOY PRESS

KANSAS, USA

Neil J Salkind is a hobbyist printer who runs Big Boy Press. He is primarily a letterpress printer, printing on a 10 x 15 Chandler & Price, a 5 x 8 Kelsey and a Vandercook Universal 1 proof press, but combines his interest in letterpress with an interest in book arts. These books were inspired by the ampersand.

The ampersand character has a most interesting history with its origins in the corruption of the Latin phrase *per se*, which would be pronounced, upon recitation, as the 27th letter of the alphabet. The recitation of "X, Y, Z *and per se and*" eventually came to be pronounced as the word "ampersand".

Its visual appearance has its founding in the *et* ligature, which was very popular when early forms of cursive were being developed.'

Salkind created many mock-ups using different type designs until the 10 final page designs were created for the accordions. A textured paper was used for the inside pages and cloth-bound book board was used for the covers.

See also:
Accordion book page 134

Purgatory Pie Press's 'InstaBook' series grew from Esther K Smith's Artist Book class. Her students' first project is to instant-publish a zine edition via photocopy or computer printer. This structure of four simple folds and a slit becomes a six-page, three-spread book with covers. Smith decided to make a set of five limited-edition instant books using real wood and metal type, and Dikko Faust's relief printing.

Shown above right are *Brains & Spines* (second from the left), letterpress-printed from photo-engravings made from Jessie Nebraska Giffords's MRI films; *Box* (third from left), a poem by Bob Holman that opens to form a box; *High Anxiety* (far right), linoleum cuts by Bill Fick which reverses to become *Team Evil* (far left); and *Gotham Golem* (second from right and below right), a manifesto that opens to show a collagraph print by London's Bob and Roberta Smith. *Enclosure Exposure* (opposite) is a collaboration with Elizabeth Duffy, who bases her artwork on the data-protection patterns from the insides of business envelopes.

See also:
Instant book page 132

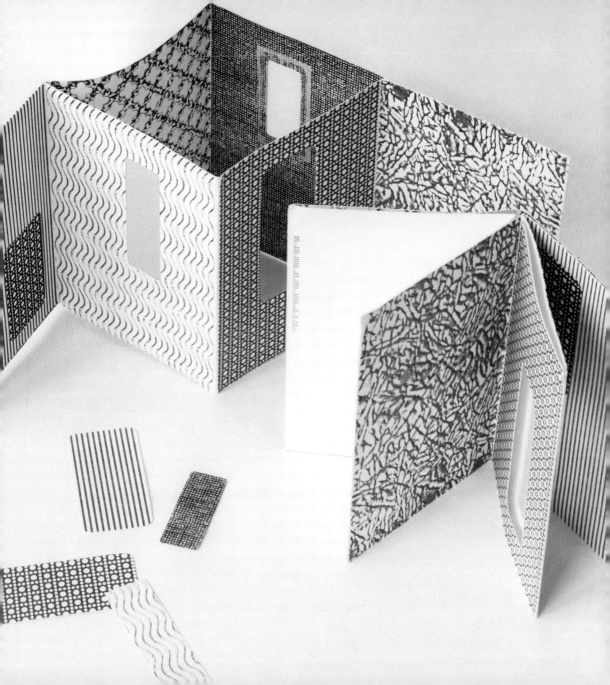

2
SEWN
BINDINGS

Sewn bindings can produce beautiful and highly decorative books. Creating them usually requires a number of tools - an awl, needle, thread - but they do not necessarily need to be too complicated. Sewn bindings not only bind the book, but they also add unique character through choice of thread and style of stitch. Some stitches are fairly simple to create, such as pamphlet stitch, while others are more elaborate, including Coptic and Secret Belgian, and while some stitches are intentionally exposed, others are hidden.

Examples in this chapter include some beautifully simple Japanese stab-stitch-bound books from Twine Bindery, experimental woven, knotted and caterpillar stitches on books by Luisa Gomes Cardoso, and Ruth Bleakley's Coptic and French Link stitch variations, all of which offer an engaging insight into the range of artisan processes involved in creating books by hand.

ALEJANDRO GRIMA CLEMENTE

For Spanish designer Alejandro Grima Clemente, book-making is something that complements his graphic design work. 'My interest in bookbinding began during my graphic design studies. I liked that I could experiment with materials, techniques, concepts and ideas without any restrictions. The creative process is what I like most about it, thinking about how to transform a concept into something tangible, into a book.'

Shown below is his *Sushi Book*, a conceptual book created with the aim of exploring the use of different types of paper combined with a range of printing techniques. The inner pages are made up of a combination of different papers - recycled papers, coloured papers, embossed papers, handmade papers, rice paper, vellum paper and coated paper - while the cover is a textured black card stock. Clemente used the Japanese stab stitch technique to bind the book.

See also:
Japanese stab stitch page 150

BOOMBOX BINDERY

Monica Holtsclaw is the bookbinder and box-maker behind Boombox Bindery. Holtsclaw works with a variety of different binding techniques, including the sewn bindings shown here.

The hardback long-stitch book (below left) was created as a Christmas gift for a friend. The pages were folded into signatures and pressed. Next, binder's board was covered with book cloth to create the hardcover and a piece of wood was cut for the spine. Sewing stations were then drilled into the wood before it was sanded and then waxed. Finally, sewing stations were punched into the folds of the signatures, and the pages and cover were sewn together through the cover and piece of wood at the same time using long stitch. Once the sewing was complete, the weaving was added to the wood for durability and aesthetics.

The book *Frontier Horizon* (below right) was created for an exhibition by the Guild of Book Workers. For this work Holtsclaw gathered a selection of mementos, resized them, made them black and white, and copied them onto vellum paper. She then folded them into sections which would represent her past, and folded blank paper into sections that would represent her future. Three sewing stations were punched into each section so she could make a series of pamphlet stitches. The pages were then stitched onto two black pieces of Cave paper. Magnets were secured between the layers of paper at each end of the binding to hold the circle shape.

See also:
Book cloth page 174
Long stitch page 148

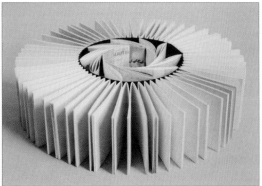

FATOS&ARTEFATOS

SÃO PAULO, BRAZIL

The bindery fatos&artefatos is run by Magda dos Santos Ribeiro, an anthropologist, crafter and book lover from São Paulo, Brazil. 'I am someone who lives surrounded by books; I love reading them, preserving them and making them. I also love papers, textures, fabrics, colours and the many possible combinations of these materials. In my anthropological research work, field notebooks are crucial, and so I decided to start making my own books using resistant materials and special papers.'

Ribeiro works using a number of different binding techniques, including many sewn bindings. Shown here is a selection of her Coptic bindings, including a Coptic cross-stitch (opposite). 'I chose to combine Coptic and French stitch because Coptic has a more resistant and smooth finish, but I wanted to use French stitch for detail and as a way of enhancing the spine of the book', she explains. 'It is not hard to do, the techniques are the same, and this is a big attraction of bookbinding; you can combine different techniques, lines, materials, papers and stitches in the same book.' Working with different patterned book cloths and brightly coloured threads, Ribero's work is beautifully bold and graphic.

See also:
Coptic stitch page 152
French link stitch page 156

CORRUPIOLA – EXPERIÊNCIAS MANUAIS

Experiências Manuais translates as 'handmade experiences' and is what the founders of Corrupiola, Leila Lampe and Aleph Ozuas, aim to create with their design and craft work. These notebooks, part of their handmade stationery, are called *Corrupios*, meaning 'a child's play' in Portuguese.

Together Lampe and Ozuas design, screenprint and bind these small notebooks one by one, using coloured Fabriano Tiziano paper for the covers and acid-free 80gsm pollen paper for signatures. Each book is hand-sewn along the spine using simple pamphlet stitch.

These mini notebooks were designed to be practical and the vivid cover colours were designed to be easily found in a purse or on a messy desk. They are made from leftover paper used for other notebooks. We like to make small products and to make the most of any paper that we have left over.'

See also:
Pamphlet stitch page 146

COFFEE MONKEY PRESS

Yuko Murata Godart of Coffee Monkey Press learnt traditional bookbinding techniques in the UK and Japan. She now resides in Los Angeles where she works as a bookbinding artist. Inspired by a love of coffee and cafés (the clue is in her choice of company name), Godart's book experiments with the conceptual side of bookbinding.

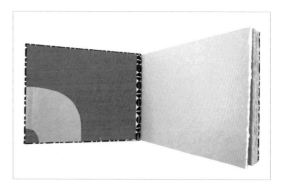

'I had a lot of fun making this. It was a combination of problem-solving, happy coincidence and pushing my desire to make a playful coffee-themed book. I wanted to somehow incorporate actual coffee beans into the book and at around the same time I was experimenting with Japanese stab binding. As much as I loved the technique, I found the spine too plain, so adding coffee beans to it was the perfect solution.'

Godart sourced fabric featuring a coffee bean-like design (actually called 'Screw head') for the cover and dyed the pages inside the book using coffee. When the book is freshly made, the smell of coffee wafts up as the pages are turned.

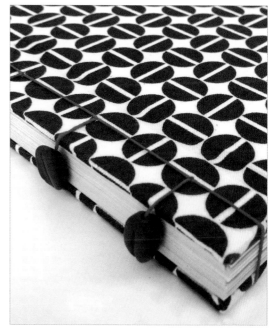

See also:
Japanese stab stitch page 150

INAYZA

Inayza is the studio name of artist and designer Gina Nagi. 'Design has been a big part of my life growing up. My work focuses mostly on detail, be it colour choice, paper textures or stitching, and I love creating unique pieces by mixing different mediums together. Through my work I want to create objects that establish a special bond between the buyer and me.'

Shown here are Nagi's books that have been bound using Coptic stitch. The sketchbook made with wrapping paper (opposite, above) contains a combination of three stitches: Coptic, kettle and long stitch. Nagi's beautiful cloth-bound board books (below, and opposite, below) are decorated with patterned paper.

Nagi works with various materials, including different papers - recycled and gift - leather, linen, threads and even lace. Each of her books is hand-sewn using linen thread. The pages within are made using Canson paper.

'The Coptic binding technique is relatively new to the Egyptian book market. I decided to use it as a way to be unique as a bookbinder here and appeal to people who would appreciate this creative form of bookbinding.'

See also:
Coptic stitch page 152
Long stitch page 148

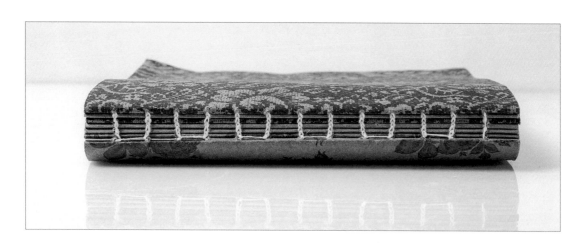

GRIMM BOOKS

BOSTON, MASSACHUSETTS, USA

Iris Grimm runs Grimm Books, a small, independent bookbindery that places an emphasis on quality craftsmanship and attention to detail. 'I strive to combine innovative design and techniques with the centuries-old art of bookbinding to create books that are modern and functional,' she explains.

Grimm specializes in hand-sewn bindings, primarily for custom-made journals, guestbooks and photo albums, as shown here. All the components for each of her books are measured and cut to size before being assembled by hand. 'I cover the boards in cloth, fold the pages, measure, mark and pierce the sewing stations on the folios and spines, and then prepare to bind them.' Her books and journals feature a variety of different stitches, including double-diamond cross-stitch, contiguous cross-stitch (below left), diamond cross-stitch, lattice stitch, long stitch and two-needle Coptic stitch (below right). Grimm uses these stitches for both their durability and aesthetic value.

'I love that I am creating things every day, and that I am making something handmade that people will use and treasure.'

See also:
Book cloth page 174
Coptic stitch page 152

RAMA

RAMA is a group of graphic designers, based in Buenos Aires, that specialize in bookbinding and letterpress printing. Shown here are examples of their sewn bindings.

The book *Ideas* (below right) features Coptic binding and a letterpress-printed cover. It is part of a series of Coptic notebooks that have covers printed with old wooden type and metal engravings.

Write It Down (above right) features Secret Belgian binding, chosen for the pattern it creates on the spine and cover. 'It is a unique and beautiful technique', say Sergio Plano and Natalia Cañas. 'With the cover we wanted to create something quiet, easy, soft and subtle, which is why we used a soft cloth with a goffering on top of it.'

The stocks used to create both books were 3mm (¹/₈in) cardboard for the covers, Bookcel 80gsm paper for the inner pages, and Fabriano 120gsm for the endpapers in *Write It Down*.

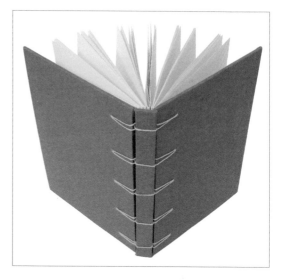

See also:
Coptic stitch page 152

ANTONIO RODRIGUES JR

Shown here is Brazilian graphic designer and illustrator Antonio Rodrigues Jr's book titled *Love*. In it he shares lyrics from one of his favourite songs, combining three of his passions - typography, craft and poetry. Fifty copies were handmade to celebrate Valentine's Day.

'I have a passion for crafts and paper. When I was a child I used to spend hours in stationery shops and warehouses. Now it has become one of my greatest (and easiest) ways to escape from a hectic day of routine.'

Rodrigues has used Japanese stab stitch to bind the book, marking the holes and then using a nail to create stations to stitch through. Cotton paper was used for the inside pages, and boards and craft paper for the cover.

See also:
Japanese stab stitch page 150

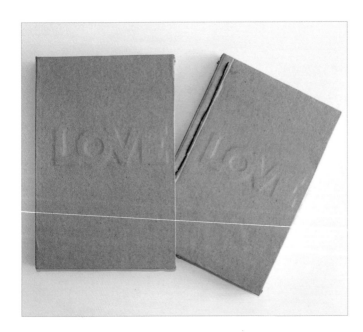

GABRIELA IRIGOYEN HANDMADE BOOKS

RIO DE JANEIRO, BRAZIL

Gabriela Irigoyen is a Rio-based designer and book-maker who takes an experimental approach to book design (see also page 16). 'I like to create books with the intention to grab people's attention. Whether that is through size, stitching or the colours I work with, I am always searching for something that will catch people's eye.'

Shown here are her takes on long-stitch binding; the star design (below right) was made by stitching a loop to hold all the threads together. These decorative stitches not only add to the aesthetics of the books, but they are also strong and durable. Both add beautiful detail to the spine. Irigoyen creates the spines using a modified Bradel technique, which gives a finer finish.

See also:
Long stitch page 148

JIANI LU

For Chinese-born Jiani Lu, a childhood spent doodling and making papercuts, jewellery and origami meant that she was always destined to have a creative career. 'I design, photograph and illustrate, and I have an unbound curiosity for new mediums and creative processes. Over the years my experience in crafts and design has translated into a key interest in package and print design, bookbinding, sewing and paper crafts. I see each new project as a learning experience, allowing me to experiment with the process, materials and aesthetics.'

Shown here are two books that she has created using Coptic and saddle stitch. *Tea-Hee* (below right), a book about the art of tea-making, features front and back covers that were handmade using canvas fabric. The pages have been divided into four signatures and bound together using Coptic stitch, which Lu chose because this allows the book to lay flat when open.

For *Window Farms* (above right and opposite), an all-in-one guide on window farming for urban farmers, Lu employed an accordion format with the five different sections (chapters) sewn together using saddle stitch. 'I used an accordion format for this book to allow for various approches to reading. When collapsed together, it reads front to back like a regular book. When expanded open, it reveals the entire length of the book with the ability to reference content from several chapters all at once.'

See also:
Accordion book page 134
Coptic stitch page 152

TWINE BINDERY

SPRING HILL, FLORIDA, USA

'I have always loved notebooks and journals and consider myself a compulsive list-maker', says Eileen Pandolfo of Twine Bindery. 'I also love to create things, so the idea of making my own journals and books is where Twine Bindery began.'

Each of Pandolfo's books are created by hand. Once the covers are designed and illustrated, she prints all the different parts of the books, punches the holes, corner-punches everything, glues the binding, adds a pocket, scores it, then binds it all together. She favours the Japanese stab stitch binding method and uses it for all her books. The covers are made using 300gsm Strathmore watercolour paper or 100 per cent recycled Kraft stock. 'I love the design process that goes into creating a notebook or journal. When I get an idea, I have to immediately drop what I'm doing and run with it. I then really enjoy going through the steps to make and perfect what I have visualized and designed.' The illustrated cover design for the *One-of-a-Kind Tribal* pocket journal (below left) was created by Pandolfo's 14-year-old daughter with a fine-tip Sharpie marker.

See also:
Japanese stab stitch page 150

SATSUKI SHIBUYA

RANCHO PALOS VERDES, CALIFORNIA, USA

Satsuki Shibuya is a designer, singer-songwriter and creative consultant based in Los Angeles. Inspired by nature and the different seasons, she created this weekly planner, which she chose to bind using buttonhole stitch. 'One of the things I associate seasonal changes with is the changing colour of leaves. I used this as my inspiration and began gathering pictures before starting to bring patterns together. I then created six different hand-drawn patterns within the book, which are graphic interpretations of leaves.'

Shibuya has used buttonhole stitch, as she wanted the book to lie flat when open. 'It is a beautiful and unique stitch, and felt like the perfect fit for the project size and function.' The cream cotton cover stock has been letterpress-printed.

SPROUTS PRESS

TORONTO, CANADA

Sprouts Press is a small press and bindery run by designer and maker Carolyn Eady from her home studio in Toronto. Her main focus is on hand-bound books, journals, sketchbooks and notebooks, created using a variety of sewn bindings, although she also loves screenprinting, drawing and painting.

For her bookbinding Eady uses new and recycled boards, found papers, handmade papers, Florentine papers, chiyogami papers and washi papers, among others.

'The functionality of the book structure and how it can be designed to suit certain activities, such as watercolour painting or writing, has shaped many of my book projects,' Eady explains. This journal is part of a series and is bound together using the Secret Belgian binding technique. She chose this technique because not only does it allow a book to be opened flat, but it also allows the front cover to flip around to the back of the book. Using the Secret Belgian binding also maximizes page use, since even the corners can be accessed.

Patterned Florentine paper has been used on the cover and is complemented with accent paper on the spine and fore edges of the cover. The cover is finished with a ribbon trim where the patterned paper meets the accent paper.

OLIVE ART

Kristi Oliver of Olive Art is both a book artist and teacher of creative arts. She started bookbinding using the Coptic method early in her teaching career and has since made hundreds of books.

'I love the finished books I create. They are like little (or sometimes big) treasures. I love seeing what people use them for and what they might include inside. I also really enjoy creating custom items to commemorate weddings and other special occasions, and trying to reflect my own self as an artist while incorporating special touches to honour the recipient of the book.'

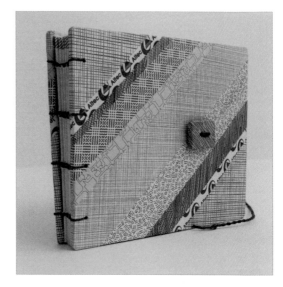

Shown here are two of Oliver's Coptic-sewn books made using a variety of different materials, including security patterns from used envelopes (above right) and nautical charts (below right). 'I created the nautical books after seeing a pile of outdated nautical charts at a boatyard. I had been using road maps for some time and have always loved the way they suggested an adventure (past or present) and an attempt to document some sort of journey, either actual or imagined.'

Oliver has used the Coptic stitch (sewn with waxed linen thread) for its strength and the fact that it allows books to lay flat when open.

See also:
Coptic stitch page 152

CANTEIRO DE ALFACES

For Rio-based bookbinder Luisa Gomes Cardoso, the art of bookbinding is all about experimentation. As well as using traditional bindings Cardoso likes to develop her own unique stitched bindings, which stem from her love of sewing.

'I learnt to sew from my mother when I was a child. My love for needlework comes from my mother and grandmothers, my love of books from my father. I began by sewing clothes but very soon I was sewing books. My main challenge with my bookbinding is to apply the techniques of sewing, embroidery and knitting that I have learnt to the art of bookbinding.'

The selected works shown here feature many different experimental bookbinding stitches, including a knitted binding (above right) and a caterpillar stitch (below right). The books shown opposite, from smallest to largest, feature ladder stitch, a pantographic binding, loop stitch and a Portuguese knotted stem stitch.

As a rule, Cardoso uses leather board for the covers of her books, which she then paints by hand with a thin layer of wax. She uses nylon, waxed or traditional embroidery threads to bind the books together.

RUTH BLEAKLEY

Florida-based designer, book artist and teacher, Ruth Bleakley (see also page 22) specializes in Coptic-bound books and variations on the Coptic stitch. 'Coptic stitch is definitely a favourite among my customers at craft shows. Most likely because it's impossible to accomplish by machine, and so you're unlikely to find it in bookshops. I enjoy using this method because it creates a journal that lays flat when it's opened, which means it's easier to write in. It's also a great-looking binding, with the braid on the outside spine of the book.'

Bleakley often uses nautical maps for the covers of her books, however she also uses washi tape (see page 22), marbling (see page 91) and other papers. 'I usually start with the cover paper first, choosing the part I'd like to make into a book, and then work back from there, deciding the eyelet colour and thread colour after the cover is cut out', she explains. The book created with a French link stitch variation (below left) was one of her first experiments in open-spine stitching. 'Normally this stitching would be hidden from view by the spine, but I thought it would look neat to show it.'

See also:
Coptic stitch page 152
French link stitch page 156
Suminagashi paper marbling page 164

ODELAE

Odelae is run by graphic designer and bookbinder Erica Ekrem from her home on Orcas Island, Washington. Ekrem's designs are largely inspired by nature, folk tales and her environment.

'Odelae journals are born from faded, timeworn materials that have survived from the early 1900s. My inspiration is discovered in old chests and bookstore salvage boxes. From materials that are no longer valued or falling apart, I reclaim what is remaining and revive it.'

Ekrem's *Field Journals* shown below were created as places to record observations in nature. The stitched star pattern on the spines was inspired by the sky at night and the idea of recording constellations within a book. The covers over the text blocks have been made using an upcycled vintage book cover, with the spines strengthened with strips of leather. The text blocks are smooth writing paper and the inner covers are lined with velvet paper. Ekrem has alternated the colour of the signatures to give the books a feeling of whimsy and playfulness. They have been stitched together using long stitch.

See also:
Long stitch page 148

HELLOJENUINE

Jen Collins, otherwise know as hellojenuine, is an illustrator working in pencil and ink, with a love of screenprinting. Shown here is one of her limited-edition hand-bound screenprinted notebooks, featuring her illustration of a perpetual bicycle. Collins has used the simple yet sturdy pamphlet stitch to bind the notebook together, which allows for the book to be opened fully flat when bound.

'Screenprinting and binding can be therapeutic processes. Although it's a time-consuming method, it means I can do each step myself from start to finish, therefore overseeing the item throughout its creation.'

Collins uses recycled card and paper supplied by Eco-Craft to create her notebooks. 'I make a point of using recycled stocks for my notebooks, as they use up more paper than other things I make, so I like that the contents are being used again. The recycled paper I use on the inside isn't so thin that drawings show through; I like that, and I like that it isn't a stark white.'

See also:
Pamphlet stitch page 146

AG&P HANDMADE

AG&P Handmade is run by freelance graphic designer Rima Bueno. Shown here are a number of her books, which feature sewn bindings - both Coptic stitch and long stitch.

'My Coptic-bound books feature a fairly utilitarian design. I like to keep them clean and simple. Because these books are intended for use as sketchbooks or creative journals, I don't want to impose a direction on the content.' Bueno has chosen Coptic stitch, as it is particularly good for sketchbooks, allowing the pages to lay flat when open.

The book *Wonderland* (above right) sees Bueno incorporate her interest in printmaking and typography into book-making. The mini books (below right) were created as experiments to test stitches, both long and Coptic.

See also:
Coptic stitch page 152
Long stitch page 148

NIGHTJAR BOOKS

TORONTO, CANADA

Bookbinder and artist Amy Egerdeen runs Nightjar Books, where she draws and creates designs for covers, makes zines, screenprints and binds books.

'I love being involved in every aspect of my work. I draw, using ink and a brush, and create patterns from my illustrations. I screenprint all my covers, brainstorm new book ideas and new designs.'

The books shown below feature Egerdeen's illustrations of houses, arrows, axes, the moon and more. She takes these illustrations and creates patterns with them in Photoshop, before making a screen from which to print onto her chosen cover stock. Once the different elements of each book are assembled she uses beeswaxed linen thread to sew them together using Coptic stitch.

'These books come from a blending of my love for Coptic-bound books and new ideas for patterns and cover designs. I really love illustrating and creating patterns for the covers of my books, and, of course, the binding itself. When I sew the signatures to the covers it is great to feel it all come together.'

See also:
Coptic stitch page 152

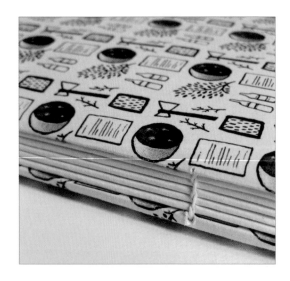

BECCA HIRSBRUNNER

Becca Hirsbrunner has bound books in a number of different styles and methods (see also page 24) but specializes in Japanese stab binding.

'I want to see how far I can push the limits of a particular style of binding, especially Japanese stab binding. I like taking a complex sketch and figuring out how to make it work within the limitations of the style. I especially enjoy creating organic designs, since most sewing patterns are strictly geometric.'

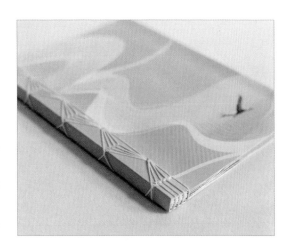

Her different stitch styles can be seen here, including a dragonfly stab pattern and a marionette pattern (both below right). There is a certain type of rhythm to complex stab binds, but once you figure that rhythm out, the design possibilities are endless. For instance, before creating the marionette stitch I had created a number of simple geometric binds using squares and single triangles. But then I thought, why not try overlapping multiple triangles together?' Hirsbrunner drills holes in her book blocks before creating her stitched patterns using waxed linen thread.

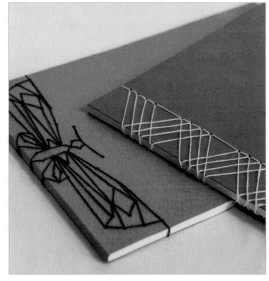

See also:
Japanese stab stitch page 150

LOUISE WALKER

MELBOURNE, AUSTRALIA

Louise Walker is a graphic designer who also works in illustration, screenprinting, typography and book-making. These days in graphic design a lot of the work requires you to use the computer. That is why I love taking any chance I can get to step away from technology and get back to the basics with crafts like bookbinding, an actual hands-on method of production.'

The travel journal shown here features Walker's design on the cover, which she affixed to craft board before assembling together with the inside pages ready for binding. She has used Coptic stitch to bind the journal, mainly for aesthetic reasons. 'I love the handmade appearance the Coptic stitch creates, and it suits the style of my travel journals perfectly. I like the fact that it gives you full control over the bind - that is, how tight the thread is, how many pages in each signature, how many holes to punch and, of course, thread colours. One thing that perhaps people do not realize is that even as the book ages, and the thread of a Coptic stitch loosens over time, the pages still stay together. The pages will never fall out.'

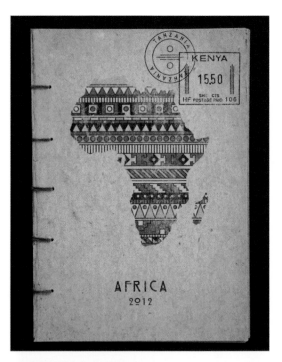

See also:
Coptic stitch page 152

GABRIELA IRIGOYEN HANDMADE BOOKS

RIO DE JANEIRO, BRAZIL

Rio-based designer and book-maker Gabriela Irigoyen (see also pages 16 and 51) experiments with a variety of sewn bindings, including the book shown here that features a technique that involves sewing raised cords onto the cover.

The signatures and the cloth-bound board covers of the book are first sewn together using Coptic stitch on the spine. Cords are then added from the back to the middle two stitches, and are then sewn around and onto the cover using embroidery thread. This technique is a way of adding beautiful texture and detail to the cover, and the cord can also be wrapped around the closed book and used to secure it. Beads have been added to the end of the cord to aid secure closure.

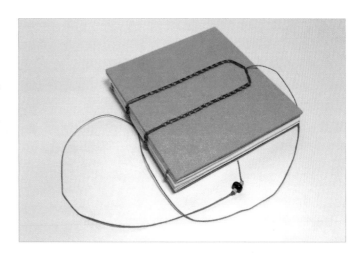

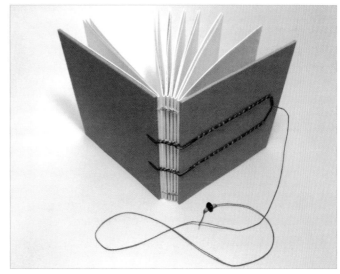

See also:
Coptic stitch page 152

WEST CERMAK

Based in Minneapolis, West Cermak is a collaboration between designer and creative Trinh Mai and artist and printer Jeffrey Nelson. With the products they create under the name West Cermak they try to combine a vareity of new and old materials, scavenging charity shops and speciality outlets for antique items, and repurposing materials that would otherwise be thrown away. The cover of the book *Mountain* (below left) features a vintage photograph of a mountain.

To bind the books they use book cloth, waxed linen thread, paper and, for some projects, screenprinting. Mai favours the use of a Coptic stitch or simple five-hole pamphlet stitch to bind her books. 'I like using these techniques because they enable me to create a visually interesting, yet clean spine, and in the case of the Coptic stitch it allows for the books to lay flat when opened.' Mai also uses reclaimed paper stocks where possible.

See also:
Book cloth page 174
Coptic stitch page 152
Pamphlet stitch page 146

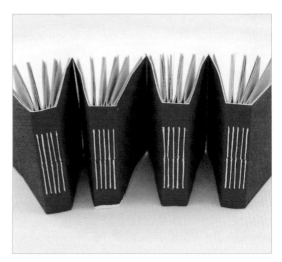

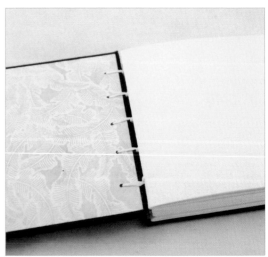

Ask for

RODKEY'S
BEST
FLOUR

EAGLE MILLING COMPANY
EDMOND, OKLA.

H&G HANDMADE

Based in Quzhou, a small city in eastern China, self-taught bookbinder Hu Jin runs H&G Handmade (see also page 87). She uses various different materials to create her books, such as linen, paper, leather, metal, clay and wood. She also likes to combine different materials and experiment with the effect these combinations have. Jin has done exactly this with the leather and linen book shown below right. She has used a simple cross pattern on the linen cover and lines on the leather spine.

Both books shown here were created by first cutting two boards for the cover and attaching them with a thick paper. The thick paper was also used to create the moulded spine. Jin then glued cloth onto the board to create the case. Once the inside pages were ready, she then bound the books using the long-stitch-binding technique.

'I chose this binding as it enables the book to be filled with many pictures without losing its shape. It also allows the spine to be as flexible as possible. When designing and making a long-stitch-bound book using leather, it is important to match your materials well. I always pay attention to the shape of the body of the book and the shape of the parts on the cover.'

See also:
Long stitch page 148

TEAM ART

Team Art is run by Amanda Lo and Charline Wang, who make paper goods, with their forte being handmade colouring books. All their humorous books are based on topics that they love, are full of puns and aim to entertain. 'The first colouring book we created was *Boy Bands: A Colouring Book.* We put it online and it quickly grew to be very popular. We decided to expand and rebrand the idea to create a set of animal and pop-culture colouring books, including ones on Jon Hamm, funny ladies and television series *Parks and Recreation, Mad Men* and *Game of Thrones.'*

Adobe Illustrator and InDesign are key programs used to create the drawings, designs and prepress work. Once all the essentials are printed, the books are individually assembled by hand. The next step is to run the books through the sewing machine to bind the pages, then the excess is trimmed with a guillotine cutter. The binding process is completed with a bellyband stamped with the title.

WINDY WEATHER BINDERY

Wendy Withrow is a bookbinder and box-maker working out of her home studio in Grand Rapids, Michigan. Through Windy Weather Bindery she aims to marry the traditional craft of bookbinding with the best of contemporary materials and design. 'I aspire to make well-crafted, utilitarian objects that are simple, beautiful and bring joy to the daily lives of others. I specialize in custom hand-bound books and boxes for a variety of clients, including photographers, designers and artists.'

Working primarily with cloth and paper, but also occasionally with leather, she case-binds many of her books using German millimetre binding. This is an elegant and clean binding that traditionally utilizes leather at the head and tail to add durability to the binding, although in Withrow's case she also uses cloth. 'I particularly like the millimetre binding because it adds strength to the corners and the head and tail, which are areas that are often damaged easily. I love the elegance of it, with the straight, clean lines as opposed to the traditional half-bindings, which cover the corners with cloth at a diagonal. I also like that it showcases the paper over the cloth.'

Withrow also favours Rubow binding, a Danish variant on millimetre binding.

See also:
Case binding page 160

SEA LEMON

Based in Phoenix, Jennifer Bates of Sea Lemon is a graphic designer by trade, but outside her full-time work as a designer she makes books and paper goods and creates online DIY projects. 'I really enjoy the process of designing a custom book, choosing the materials and exploring binding methods to make a unique, functional book. I like to work with a variety of papers and threads to create unique or modified stitch bindings.'

The case-bound books shown here were created to be used as journals or sketchbooks. To make the books Bates first created the text blocks and then used the cover paper to make decorative headbands. These headbands have been glued directly onto the spine of the text block.

The case, or cover, is made using a corresponding decorative paper. The paper is applied to book board and then the text block is glued into the case.

See also:
Case binding page 160

3
PAGE AND COVER TREATMENTS

Throughout this chapter we look at the different ways in which book-makers treat the inside pages and covers of their books. From experimenting with food dyes to marbling and hand-stamping, the ways in which they work to change and manipulate the materials they use is varied. Some techniques are more complex than others, but all have the same result, which is to add character, texture or colour to the handmade books.

New York-based artist Natalie Stopka's work is material driven, and in this chapter we look at her plant-dyed linen book covers as well as her hand-stitched embellishments. We also look at Ruth Bleakley's marbled covers and Lotta Hellberg's eco-printed and indigo-dyed covers. These and other contemporary examples showcase the beautiful results that can be achieved with each technique.

ANNA FEWSTER

KENT, UK

Anna Fewster runs a small press producing limited-edition literary material on an Adana Eight-Five letterpress printer from a cottage on England's east Kent coast. Her focus is on texture and colour.

'I like to create work that expresses and reflects my love of design and detail, and that inspires an appreciation of the characteristic texture and quality of letterpress.'

Fewster has used marbling to bring colour and texture to this book cover. She experimented for some weeks before settling on the right colours and look. Fewster uses watercolours floated in carrageenan to create the marbled effect, which is a messy, traditional method that yields very vivid results. 'Marbling has a lovely loose spontaneity to it, and each cover is completely unique.'

Fewster used off-white Zerkall mould-made 145gsm stock for the inside pages, which were letterpress printed, and a smooth Somerset 200gsm for the cover, as clear and clean marbling needs a smooth surface. The book was then bound using pamphlet stitch with linen thread.

See also:
Pamphlet stitch page 146
Suminagashi paper marbling page 164

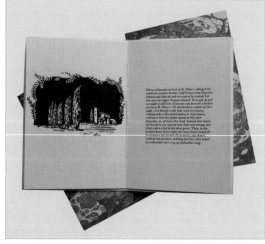

ALICE FOX

Alice Fox is a visual artist working in textiles and printmaking, taking much of her inspiration from the natural world. With a previous career in conservation, Fox aims to use sustainable processes in her work to celebrate the natural world, while at the same time having minimum impact upon it.

'I work with paper, linen, silk and wool. I often treat paper as a textile, stitching into it and dyeing it in the same way I would a piece of fabric.'

The series 'Tide Marks', shown here, was inspired by coastal landscapes and serves as a record of Fox's beach walks. To create the effect on the pages in the books, Fox first used tea to stain the paper, then soaked it, before making collagraph prints using a printing press and plates made with found items. Fabriano Rosaspina paper was used for the inside pages because it can withstand the fairly deep embossing from the collagraph print. Grey boards covered in cotton bookbinding cloth have been used for the covers.

'These books are records of my walks on the beach. They can be seen as snapshots of moments, textures and marks from the beach captured in a linear form.'

See also:
Accordion book page 134

SCANTRON PRESS

Nourish, All Our Relations, by Diane Jacobs of Scantron Press, celebrates the wonders of our natural and man-made world. Beneath the beauty, however, lies an environmental time bomb of catastrophic proportions. Through seduction and metaphor, Jacobs weaves layered imagery to awaken a sense of urgency. It is an unbound artist book composed of eight twice-folded folios, printed on both sides, and housed in a hand-crafted collapsible bamboo box. She mapped out 15 different multicolour reduction relief prints, printed polymer plates made from drawings and then utilized pressure-printing methods. The pages have endured more than 100 runs through a Vandercook letterpress.

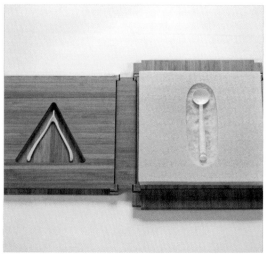

While working on *Nourish*, Jacobs discovered that transparent paper introduces an element of artistic chance. As light shines through a page, layers of colour and image become much more than the sum of their parts; they reveal new meanings. The papers used were Gampi-shi, two-layer Gampi and Usuyo Gampi. The bamboo box contains a porcelain wishbone and a cast paper-pulp spoon, sewn onto wool felt.

SERENA OLIVIERI

Serena Olivieri is an Italian illustrator now based in Madrid, Spain. She is a self-taught book-maker with a passion for pattern design, who always likes to experiment with new techniques. Her handmade notebooks feature plenty of patterns, colour cut-outs and pop-ups.

'I love the process involved in making these books. Each time I start a new book I find a way to make something different within it. I love to go to the paper shop and to choose between the different textures of paper.'

Flores (right) features hand-drawn illustrations on the cover, the edges of which have been cut out. 'I wanted to create a decoration for the cover so began by drawing flowers. I wasn't convinced, though, so decided to cut out pieces from the edge,' Olivieri explains. This book has been Italian bound, another example of simple sewn binding.

ANNEKE DE CLERCK

Anneke De Clerck (see also page 20), has created this set of six books that all incorporate hand-stamping on the cover.

'I found this photorealistic rose stamp by Darkroom Door and when I started stamping with it to find the right colour, the idea was born to make a series of six books.' The result is a set of six different coloured stamped books that sit inside a handmade box.

De Clerck has used Coptic stitch to bind the books. 'I love this stitch; I used it to make my first book. It is great because, as it lies flat when open, it makes it easier to paint, draw and write in the book.'

The covers were made from a cream coloured medium-weight smooth paper and De Clerck chose a handmade paper to cover the box.

See also:
Coptic stitch page 152

CATHY DURSO

Specializing in embroidered covers, Cathy Durso is a Boston-based artist and bookbinder who makes hand-bound journals, sketchbooks, portfolio cases and keepsake boxes. She creates custom-made books and box covers featuring embroidered images, monograms, names, dates and phrases, among others.

'My main clients are artists looking for a custom portfolio case, as well as people looking to give a special keepsake gift to an artist or writer. I enjoy the duality of creativity and meticulous attention to detail that bookbinding requires, and I really love transforming my customers' ideas into a finished product that they love and treasure.'

Largely inspired by science and nature, Durso draws out a design on the reverse side of her cloth, which she uses as a guide for the stitching. After the design is stitched onto the cloth, the cloth is glued to the book board. For closed-spine books she uses traditional Western-style multi-signature binding for its strength and durability - ideal for books that get a lot of use, such as journals and sketchbooks.

See also:
Book cloth page 174

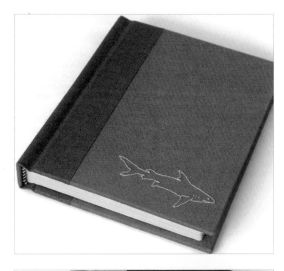

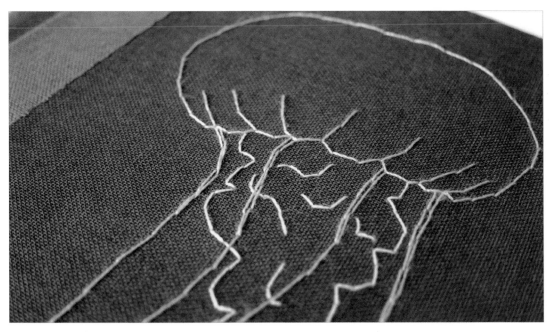

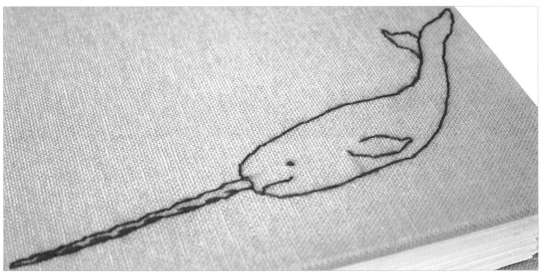

INAYZA

Inayza is the studio name of Cairo-based artist and designer Gina Nagi (see also page 46). She is experimental in her work, as can be seen here with these cover designs.

The embroidered book (centre right) was created for a Christmas bazaar and sees the stitches follow onto the cover from the Coptic-stitched spine. Nagi punched 2mm ($\frac{1}{12}$in) holes into the cover first so she could stitch through them using linen thread.

For the hand-printed cover (above right), Nagi created patterns using vegetable stamps made from potatoes, carrots and peppers, as well as old sweet wrappers. Canson paper stock was used for the cover of this simple pamphlet-sewn notebook.

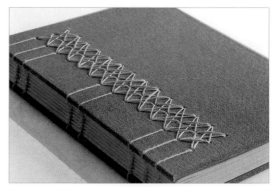

The marbled cover (below right) was created for a client who was particulary interested in marbling. Nagi teamed the traditional, old-style marbling technique with a brightly coloured modern cloth on the spine. The book was stitched using linen thread, gauze and craft paper, and features a fabric band to strengthen the spine.

See also:
Coptic stitch page 152
Pamphlet stitch page 146
Suminagashi paper marbling page 164

H&G HANDMADE

Self-taught bookbinder Hu Jin runs H&G Handmade in Quzhou in eastern China (see also page 72). Jin designs her own patterns, which she prints on book cloth. The pattern designs are based on a variety of inspirations, but particularly trees and flowers.

'Nature always inspires me. The patterns I create take me back to certain places, like lying on the grass, hearing the sounds of leaves and branches swaying in the wind above me.'

Jin has screenprinted each of the covers shown below by hand. The linen cloth is then fixed to book boards and assembled with the signatures before being bound together. Jin uses Coptic stitch, 'a simple and elegant binding that allows the patterns on the cover to be completely visible. I think the cover and the stitch also complement each other really well.'

See also:
Book cloth page 174
Coptic stitch page 152

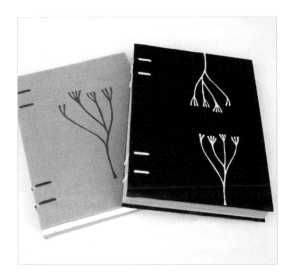

INK+WIT

FAYETTEVILLE, NEW YORK, USA

Tara Hogan, the founder of INK+WIT, is a graphic designer and illustrator who specializes in brand identity, stationery design and limited-edition printing. She favours working with letterpress, wood veneer and screenprinting, and likes to experiment with materials and textures.

The book shown below was created as a personal project dedicated to her grandfather and his love of the outdoors and nature. Hogan carried out extensive photo research and scanned images into Adobe Illustrator to create a collage and add type. She also researched different papers and textures.

The book was bound using pamphlet stitch with a natural embroidery thread. 'The book-making process has so many layers,' Hogan explains. 'Your appreciation for books is heightened when you see how much work is involved precision-wise and time-wise.'

See also:
Pamphlet stitch page 146

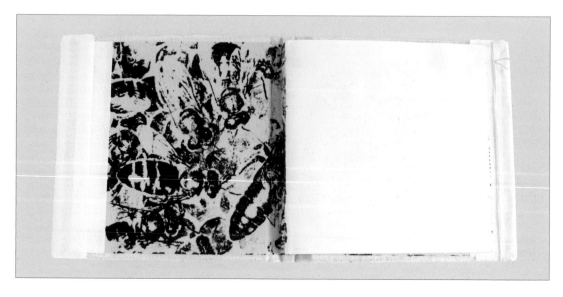

LOTTA HELLEBERG

Born in Sweden, Lotta Helleberg is a textile artist, printmaker and self-taught book artist. She uses hand-printed and hand-dyed fabrics as a base for quilts, collages and other objects.

'I love how handmade books can tell a story, without always using a lot of words. I have always loved making work that is both beautiful and useful, and that is how these small notebooks came to be.'

These notebooks (right) feature eco-printed and indigo-dyed covers. Eco-printing is achieved by layering paper (or fabric) with plants, then either rolling or clamping them tight and exposing them to simmering water or steam. Indigo-dyeing is another natural dye method, but it is faster because it simply involves dipping paper in an indigo vat several times to create subtle colour variations and lines.

See also:
Natural plant dyeing page 172

RAMA

Argentinian graphic design group RAMA specialize in bookbinding and letterpress printing (see also page 49). Their focus is on colour, typography and experimenting with different materials. Their work often features different kinds of papers, cardboards and fabrics, as well as various recycled materials including old magazines and newspapers, plastics and wood.

Shown here is their case-bound notebook *Rainy Days*, a one-of-a-kind book made using Bookcel 80gsm stock for the inner pages, Fabriano 120gsm stock for the endpapers and 3mm (⅛in) cardboard for the cover. The cover has been finished with white bookbinding cloth that has been hand-painted with both fabric paint and acrylics.

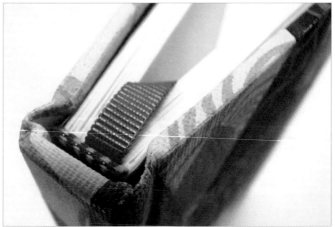

See also:
Book cloth page 174

RUTH BLEAKLEY

As well as making Coptic-bound books, designer, book artist and teacher Ruth Bleakley (see also pages 22 and 60) specializes in making marbled paper.

'Marbling is a very old method of decorating paper using floating inks or paints on a liquid surface. By laying a sheet of paper on top of these floating inks and pulling a one-time print off the surface, you have your marbled paper.'

Bleakley's favoured marbling technique is the Japanese technique of floating black Sumi-e ink on water to create designs that look like woodgrain, with thick alternating black and white rings. Once they are dry, Bleakley uses the marbled papers to cover her Coptic-bound books. She also creates marbled papers using coloured inks.

See also:
Coptic stitch page 152
Suminagashi paper marbling page 164

FEEDING THE LAKE

LINCOLN, NEBRASKA, USA

Katie Taylor Frisch of Feeding the Lake is a fibre artist and bookbinder working with felted wools and handmade paper. She uses a range of techniques to create cover material for her hand-bound books.

The cover shown here was created with fibre-reactive dyes, which are synthetic dyes that bond with fibre. Taylor Frisch also uses linen fabrics which she block-prints, and she works with handmade pigmented cotton paper stocks. The interior pages of her books are either handmade recycled stocks or 80gsm Neenah Environment stock.

'I create my books and journals out of my love for textiles. I also love creating books, beautiful vessels for the recording of wisdom and experiences.'

See also:
Book cloth page 174

COLDSNAP BINDERY

Originally from Canada but now based in Berlin, Leah Buckareff is a bookbinder who primarily creates case-bound books, she likes to print, paint and embroider her designs onto the cloth she uses to cover her books.

'I generally find inspiration in my travels (abstract landscapes) or in the particular paper or cloth I'll be using. This makes each of my books 'one of a kind' . . . I repeat motifs, but the characteristics of the material and the fact it's all completely handmade means that no two books are exactly alike.'

Little Trees (above and centre right) features a linen cloth cover embroidered with small pine trees. Buckareff used an accordion-fold binding to create the book, with the pages made using acid-free Canson paper.

I Used to be Wood (below right) is a pamphlet-stitched book that features Buckareff's embroidery. Inspired by the woodgrain paper she used for the cover, the journals have a message: 'I wanted people who consume books and journals to remember where the material they are made with comes from, and consider this. I guess I'm sharing my guilt with a little humour.' Buckareff has painted the paper edges of the book with watercolours that match the colour of the threads used in the cover embroidery.

See also:
Pamphlet stitch page 146

PAINTED FISH STUDIO

SAINT PAUL, MINNESOTA, USA

Designer Jen Shaffer of Painted Fish Studio created these two hand-punched books in her home studio in Minnesota. Book covers such as these are made using cloth-covered board; Shaffer then uses a book drill to punch the letters into the covers based on a paper template she creates. An interior cover sheet is glued to the boards and, after drying, the inside signatures are either glued or bound to the covers, depending on the book type.

'Paper is my favourite material to work with, but I'm always looking for ways to make it unique. I like to use unexpected embellishments or colour combinations. Sometimes I wonder if my love of bookbinding is an excuse to justify buying the lovely papers I find.'

For the book *Hi* (above right) she has used matt board and pink book cloth for the cover, and Arches watercolour paper for the inside pages. The cover of *Hello* (below right) is made of matt board covered with off-white book cloth, and the inside pages are French's Dur-O-Tone Newsprint Extra White.

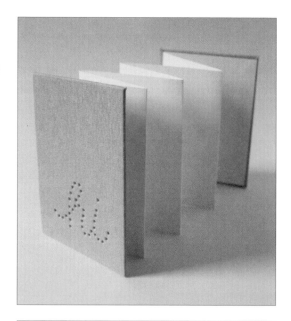

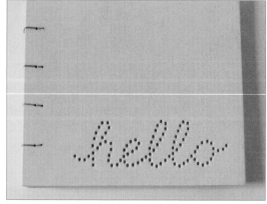

See also:
Book cloth page 174

EMMA BONSALL

Emma Bonsall is an English crafter and maker based in Canada, who specializes in using recycled materials. Her favoured materials for decorative book-making are vintage atlases, geography textbooks, tourist maps and old subway maps. 'Discarded maps have such a beauty of shape and colour and history to them that I am constantly rescuing them. Being able to take a basic notebook and turn it into something desirable using recycled materials seems the perfect fit for me.'

The *Atlas* cover (below right) was created with recycled pages from a 1970s *National Geographic* atlas, woven together to create a 'fabric' that was then stuck to the book cover. The pattern-covered books (below left) have been created using recycled security envelopes. Bonsall cut, folded and played with the security papers, separating out the colours and patterns, and finding complementary designs to work with. There are so many different colour and pattern combinations with security envelopes, commonly geometric designs that lend themselves so well to modern creative works. I love the idea of people saving and using their own security envelopes, a plentiful, free source of decorative papers given to everyone.'

See also:
Woven cover page 176

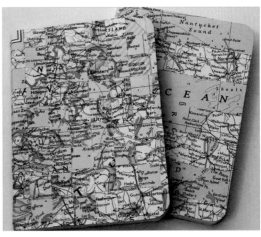

MARJOLEIN COENRADY

Marjolein Coenrady is a graphic designer from the Netherlands with a passion for book design, bookbinding, paper and typography. She created these books to have a handmade, unique look on the outside, and to be functional on the inside - ruled pages for the notebooks (below right and opposite) and blank paper for the sketchbook (above right). The covers of these books feature images created from dried plants that she found in her mother's old school books.

'The plant specimens I found in the old books were stunning; so carefully preserved with old pieces of tape that had turned sepia in colour with age. I scanned the best pages and made a series of paper goods out of them, which I then used on the covers of these notebooks.'

Coenrady's books have linen spines, and in the case of the sketchbook, a ribbon closure. The pages of the sketchbook are glued together so that it is possible for users to easily tear out their sketches.

AG&P HANDMADE

Freelance graphic designer Rima Bueno runs AG&P Handmade (see also page 64) and uses bookbinding as a way of escaping from the computer and utilizing her creativity.

'I like to follow things that interest me and have fun with them. With bookbinding I really wanted to make something useful out of the excess paper samples and supplies that have accumulated from my print work. I love playing with paper and materials, experimenting with their properties and pulling together different colours and textures.'

Bueno's Unryu paper case-bound books feature a number of different leftover papers with varying textures and colours. These Unryu papers are soft, cloth-like papers that also have varied translucence. The cases were covered with coloured papers first, so the Unryu papers wouldn't be dulled down by the brown boards showing through.

See also:
Case binding page 160

Based in North London, Harrington & Squires is run by designers and printers Chrissie Charlton and Vicky Fullick. Together they create bespoke design and letterpress prints, products and limited-edition books. They also run workshops where they teach typography, typesetting and letterpress printing.

Shown here are two of their handmade books, *The Jealous Sole* (below left) and *In Art* (above and below right). Both books feature pierced and punched inner pages. For *The Jealous Sole*, Charlton and Fullick worked into the pages of the book using various perforators, cutters and hole punchers to add another dimension to the surface of the paper. Similarly, for *In Art*, the surface of the paper was worked into using a Japanese screw punch, to create lines of holes to connect the type and add another element to the illustration. Both books were bound by hand in a style that replicates machine-stitching on fabric.

PAPERIAARRE

JYVÄSKYLÄ, FINLAND

Kaija Rantakari is a bookbinder and artist based in Jyväskylä, Finland. Many of her books feature Coptic binding. 'I love the simplicity of the structure, how it's stripped down to the mere essentials. It's easy to combine this simple structure with simple, stylish materials.'

Rantakari is particularly keen on using fabric covers, which she adorns with vintage finds or embroidery. She tends to begin the creative process by finding materials that inspire her before then going ahead to design and create a book. The books included here feature pieces of delicate lace material, linen fabric and antique brass discs on the covers.

'More often than not I use linen as my covering material; it's a beautiful fabric on its own, but it's also a wonderful background for all sorts of things, like vintage bits and bobs, or embroidery. I like how linen gives a book an ageless look that can be manipulated into the direction of modern as well as the style of some long-gone era.'

See also:
Book cloth page 174
Coptic stitch page 152

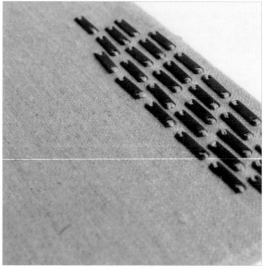

NATALIE STOPKA

New York-based Natalie Stopka would describe herself as a book artist focused on unconventional structure, textiles and tactility.

'My work is very materials-driven, and so I enjoy the exploratory process at the beginning of a project. I focus on working with uncommon fibres, repurposed and hand-dyed fabrics, and vintage textiles. This can include everything from dyeing and eco-printing to weaving and embroidery.'

The linen cover, pages, binding thread and silk headbands of each of the case-bound books shown here (above and below right, and opposite top left) have been naturally dyed with plant materials. Each of these fibres takes the same dye in a distinctly different shade, showing the range of colours that can be achieved from dyeing different materials with the same plant. The dye from the plants is extracted by soaking or simmering. Each of the elements of the books are then mordanted with alum to assist the dye in bonding to the fabric and paper fibres. The fabric and papers are then submerged in the dye bath for at least 24 hours. Once rinsed and dried they are ready for binding.

Stopka's other covers (opposite top right and below) feature not only embroidery techniques but also sculpted fabric, which is sewn into place by hand using French knot stitches.

See also:
Natural plant dyeing page 172

PAGE AND COVER TREATMENTS 103

4
EXPERIMENTAL PACKAGING

Experimenting with the cover, or 'packaging', of a given book is a great way to make it stand out and give it that something extra.

All of the books in this chapter feature materials or techniques that aim to achieve exactly this. From André Lee Bassuet of Kowaikuma's pillow books, to Norman Pointer's beautifully crafted wood-covered books, to Larissa Cox of Boundless Bookbindery's cake books and Erica Ekrem of Odelae's clam-shell cases, each pushes the boundaries of design and experimentation. In some cases, these covers, and others on the following pages, took the makers many days to create. From finding the right materials to practising and perfecting the binding and finishing techniques, they illustrate the intriguing creative possibilities of book-making as an art form.

THREE TREES BINDERY

CHARLOTTE, NORTH CAROLINA, USA

Three Trees Bindery began as a marriage of two of Michelle Skiba's favourite things: trees and books.

'As an avid journal keeper and book collector, creating books from things found in the forest evolved slowly and naturally from my wanderings. Completely taken with the beauty of an acorn, a leaf or a piece of bark, I was unable to put down these small tokens and they became the source of inspiration for my wooden library.'

Skiba specializes in creating wooden wedding guestbooks and photo albums. She begins her design process by selecting her wood and bark. The goal of her process is to highlight the wood's natural and organic beauty, which often means highlighting flaws and imperfections. 'To me these are the characteristics that make these materials unique. I sand and shape the boards, then use wax, paints and natural oil finishes.'

To bind the books she uses a slight variation on the traditional Coptic binding. She developed it by changing some of the stitches to create the woven pattern along the spine. 'I love the juxtaposition of the simple and rustic covers with the care and precision of the exposed sewing.'

See also:
Coptic stitch page 152

JULIA NITZSCHE

YAOUNDÉ, CAMEROON

Currently living and working in Cameroon, book artist Julia Nitzsche created the covers for the books shown here using salvaged scraps of fabric. She works with locally acquired printed 'pagnes', a traditional garment worn by women, as well as a fine cotton called Bazin Riche, which is used for batik and hand-dyeing.

Nitzsche has the pieces of fabric treated using a specially developed coating to strengthen and protect them and facilitate the weaving technique. She also creates book covers using a geometric quilting technique where she places covered boards on top of one another, mixing different fabrics together (opposite).

'With the woven patterns I like to see what happens when two fabrics are interacting. Since they are large and high contrast, there is an interesting play between the two fabrics and the more rectilinear design of the weaving. I also like the fact that as the larger patterns are interrupted by the weaving, the mind's eye completes the motifs. With the geometric covers, many types of fabric can be used to cover the boards, and it is in the mix of fabrics that a new type of imagery emerges on the covers.'

See also:
Woven cover page 176

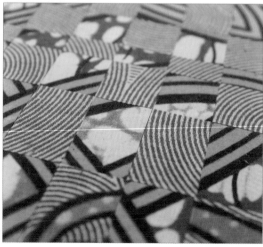

KILLSIDE KRAFTS

TORONTO, CANADA

Killside Krafts is run by bookbinder Melodie Kwan, who makes Coptic-bound journals and blackboard-inspired handmade goods. She works with Baltic birch plywood, book board, linen and cotton fabrics, and various papers and elastics when creating her books.

Inspired by early Coptic bindings, which had wooden boards as covers, Kwan found Baltic birch plywood to be a good alternative. It retains the look of solid wood with the woodgrain pattern on both sides, while being around the same thickness as book board, making it ideal for covers.

In some instances, Kwan then laser-cuts designs into the cover before assembling all the different book elements together and binding them using Coptic stitch.

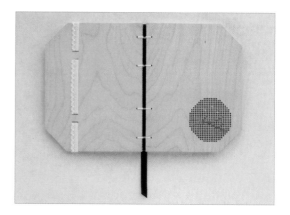

See also:
Coptic stitch page 152

IMMAGINACIJA

Lucie Forejtová is the artist behind Immaginacija and works as an artisan stationer from her home workshop in Oxford.

'Immaginacija means imagination; even though it is a made-up word and doesn't come from any particular language, I believe it's understandable in all languages. My work is all about imagination, and about the imagination of my customers who commission me to create bespoke books. I specialize in making notebooks and journals, but I also create special bindings, limited or special editions of books - poetry pamphlets, for instance.'

Forejtová uses a variety of different styles and materials within her work, including handmade and recycled materials. Shown here are her books with woven (above right) and patchwork (below right) covers, which have an emphasis on colour.

To create the woven book Forejtová used strips of various types of papers - handmade, decorative, painted, marbled - to create a woven sheet of paper, which she then used to cover the book board. The patchwork book was created using recycled paper left over from other projects. The books were bound using Coptic stitch.

See also:
Coptic stitch page 152
Woven cover page 176

KOWAIKUMA

Kowaikuma is run by Brooklyn artist André Lee Bassuet. *Kowai kuma*, meaning 'scary bear,' was a nickname given to Bassuet while she was studying in Japan: 'I loved to hibernate in the winter like a bear and I would get scary without food, sleep or art. I love to be creatively challenged every day,' she says.

Japan is an influence that features in much of Bassuet's work. The book covers shown here are made from vintage kimonos that have been upcycled into book cloth. The pillow books (below right) are a play on a well-known eleventh-century Japanese book of thoughts, poetry and musings by Sei Shōnagon. A court lady to Empress Consort Teishi, Shōnagon wrote on sheets that she kept under her pillow, hence the name. Bassuet has created a more literal interpretation with the covers of her pillow books.

Bassuet favours Coptic stitch for the binding as she can sew messages onto the spine. *XOXO* (above right) is intended to be a gift for a loved one, or a romantic journal.

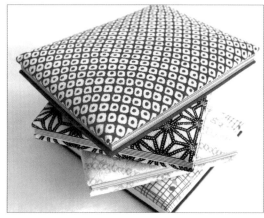

See also:
Book cloth page 174
Pillow book page 180

CHRISTER DAHLSLETT

ALTA, NORWAY

Christer Dahlslett is a graphic designer who, in his own words, likes to work with whatever materials he can get his hands on. As a freelancer he travels around, staying a month or two in different cities before moving on to a new, exciting place. He was attracted to the world of design because of the opportunities to experiment. 'I love that I can play around with almost anything. I enjoy experimenting with new materials, new techniques and new tools, although I always keep in mind what the specific materials and techniques I use will communicate.'

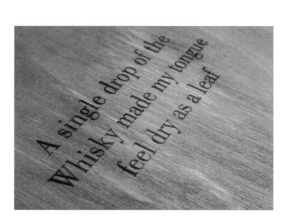

Dahlslett's book *The Water of Life* was created as part of his design degree and explores the world of whisky drinking, particularly the 'manly' side of it. The book features three individual pamphlet-stitched books housed inside a case made from plywood. 'Since this book was about a very "manly" drink, I wanted to create a cover that was robust and sturdy. I used plywood which I had laser-cut. Once cut, I sanded it down, applied different dyes to stain it and then glued it together to form the case,' he explains.

The text has been burnt onto the wood with a laser-cutter, which was also used to cut out the box. Dahlslett used 3mm (⅛in) plywood for the case and three different stocks for the pamphlet-stitched books: 180gsm watercolour stock, a 150gsm stock and a 110gsm off-white stock.

See also:
Pamphlet stitch page 146

EWELINA ROSINSKA

ŁÓDŹ, POLAND / LONDON, UK

Ewelina Rosinska is a Polish-born graphic designer working across all areas of design, from web design to handcrafted objects.

Shown here is her portfolio, which she created to show her eclectic work together in one place. The hand-bound book also features printed images of her work that have been stitched together before being bound by a board cover. Rosinska chose a patterned design (below right) for her endpapers and case lining to make her portfolio distinctive. 'With the creation of this book I wanted to make something personal, and something that showed I care about the details within design,' she explains.

The book is secured with a ribbon and housed inside a cardboard case, which is secured with another ribbon.

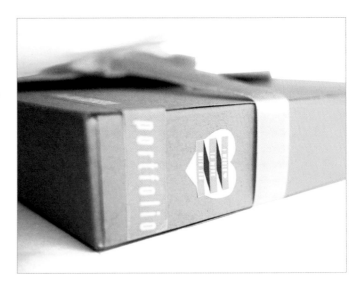

LIME RIOT

Mareth Cordell is the woman behind Seattle-based company Lime Riot. As a maker she dabbles in many different crafts, including knitting, embroidery, sewing, paper crafts, painting and clay, but she is always interested in trying something new.

As an avid list-maker, Cordell was inspired to create covers for the journals and books that she uses to capture her lists, ideas and inspirations. The fabric covers she creates are removable so they can be used multiple times on different books or journals.

Each book cover is made using carefully selected complementary fabrics, which Cordell sews together on her sewing machine. She stamps a Dewey Decimal library code on the covers to help her identify the purpose of the book, be it for recipes, lists, decorating ideas, sewing, knitting, crafting and so on.

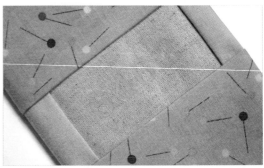

See also:
Fabric cover page 178

NORMAN POINTER

BARDSTOWN, KENTUCKY, USA

Book artist Norman Pointer is a retired physician who now spends his time creating handmade books made with aged and prepared wood that he collects – in some instances, from trees that he has felled himself. The woods Pointer uses include sumac, Californian redwood, hackberry, black walnut, wild grape, holly and bald cypress.

'Because I live near Louisville and the Ohio River I have access to the driftwood that collects at the Falls of the Ohio. This is a good source of material for me, and one of my ongoing projects is making a collection of books using native American woods.'

Once the wood is collected and prepared for use, Pointer cuts it to size and drills holes in it ready for stitching. He then sands it before he begins sewing his prepared signatures to the cover using Irish waxed linen and Coptic stitch.

See also:
Coptic stitch page 152

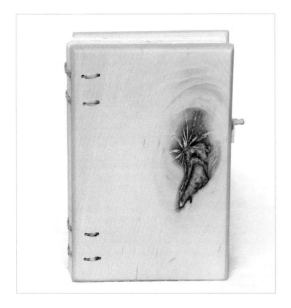

BOUNDLESS BOOKBINDERY

VIENNA, AUSTRIA

Originally from Bath, England, book artist Larissa Cox now resides in Vienna where she creates beautiful hand-bound books under the name Boundless Bookbindery. These 'cake books' were inspired by the city.

'Living as I do in Vienna, home of splendid cakes, it seemed natural to take inspiration from this tradition and create cakes in book form. My aim was to give the books as close an appearance to an actual cake as possible, while still being fully functioning books. Thus they all have the dimensions of a real (quite generous) cake slice.'

Each of the books were case-bound in a normal rectangular shape and then hand-cut into a triangular shape. Cox then added the covers and hand-stitched headbands. The inner pages of the cake books are Fabriano Tiziano stock and the covers are made with either bookbinding linen or decorative paper.

See also:
Case binding page 160

HINGED STRUNG STITCHED

PORTLAND, OREGON, USA

Run by Molly Lewis and Michelle Johnson, Hinged Strung Stitched is a small Portland-based bookbinding studio, specializing in custom photo albums and one-of-a-kind books, boxes and portfolios. 'We are working to keep the traditional art of bookbinding alive and thriving', they say.

The architecture portfolio book (opposite), created for Matt Fuhr, features a Coptic binding and a laser-etched cedar wood cover. The design of the tri-fold book (right) is based on the traditional gatefold binding that Lewis and Johnson modified to create a book that is completely self-contained without requiring a slipcase. 'The book is bound using simple pamphlet stitch. Multiple signatures make the binding look elegant and architectural . . . we refer to it as a long-stitch binding because it better describes what the binding actually looks like.'

See also:
Coptic stitch page 152
Pamphlet stitch page 146

ASKIDA

Askida was founded by Özlem Kumru who designs and makes hand-bound books and accessories, including bags and hats. Her decorative book covers are mostly made using balsa wood as a base, and then decorated with various materials and objects. 'I love to use an unusual harmony in contradictory objects - such as felts, found objects, gemstones or beads - to create "scenery" on the cover.'

Kumru is a self-taught bookbinder who began researching historical bookbinding techniques after she graduated. She uses 160gsm Canson paper for the inside pages of her books and stitches her chosen objects onto 4mm ($^3/_{16}$in) balsa wood covers using cotton thread. Kumru binds her books with various stitches, including Secret Belgian and Coptic, using either waxed cotton thread, raffia straw thread or cord.

'I love the pattern that the thread creates on the cover and spine when using the Secret Belgian binding technique. However, I tend to use Coptic stitch on the smaller books I make, simply because of the smaller dimensions.'

See also:
Coptic stitch page 152

ODELAE

Graphic designer and bookbinder Erica Ekrem of Odelae (see also page 62) says: 'I strive to live in harmony with my environment and find myself continually seeking a balance between the natural world and the one created by mankind. I work with found materials - mostly vintage and natural objects, such as clam shells and driftwood.'

The idea for the shell book shown here came from a walk on the beach. Part of a series, the first book was made from a clam shell, but Ekrem has since used scallop, cockle and oyster shells. The text block was created using smooth, white, 100 per cent recycled writing paper. It was assembled together with the shells, which were pre-drilled with holes, ready for attaching to the text block, and bound using Coptic stitch and linen thread.

Ekrem chose Coptic stitch because it reflects the simplicity and humbleness of the shells she repurposes. As they are non-adhesive, the shell books are 100 per cent biodegradable.

See also:
Coptic stitch page 152

5
BOOK-MAKING IN PRACTICE

While the previous chapters in this book offer inspiration, this final chapter provides you with practical instruction and advice on how to master an extensive variety of different binding techniques. Some are more in-depth than others, and some require more materials and tools, but all are accessible and give both beginners and more advanced book-makers the chance to create a series of unique and individual books.

These illustrated step-by-step tutorials take you though a range of techniques, from the fairly simple accordion fold to the more complex carousel fold, and from the basic pamphlet stitch to the more advanced French link and Coptic stitches, as well as instructions on how to case-bind a book. This final chapter also explores different techniques for decorating papers, as well as suggestions for how to accomplish a range of eye-catching cover treatments, including Suminagashi paper marbling, frottage and natural plant-dyeing techniques.

TOOLS AND MATERIALS

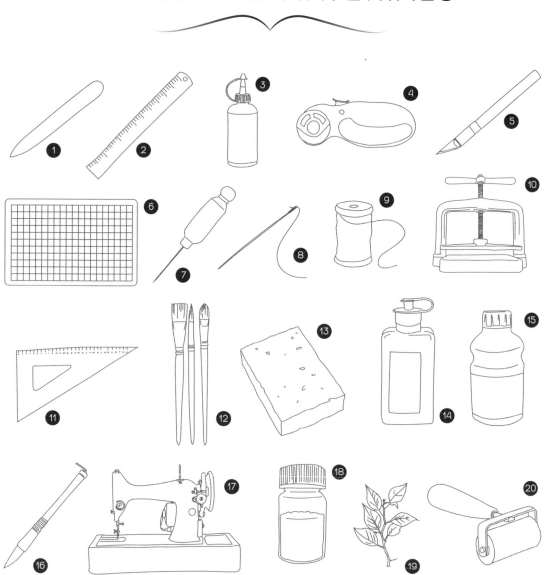

Paper Good art papers are often made from cotton or linen rags. Try a variety and see what you like that suits your budget. Beware of high-acid papers, such as newsprint and children's construction paper - they are too brittle for bookbinding. Many different weights of paper are available, and papers are sized for different processes.

Decorative paper is great for endsheets or covering book boards. A variety of decorative papers are available at good art shops, including marbled, textured, coloured or Japanese papers. Some wrapping papers are high quality, but beware of brittle papers that might tear as you fold them. Alternatively you can make your own decorative paper, such as paste paper (see page 168), marbled paper (see page 164) or frottage paper (see page 170).

Kozo paper Often incorrectly referred to as rice paper, Kozo paper, from Japan, Thailand and Korea, is strong, thin paper with long fibres. It is good for backing cloth and mending, as well as for book pages.

Yasutomo's Hosho Sumi sketch paper This is one paper that you could use for Suminagashi paper marbling (see page 164).

Book board Also known as binder's board, book board is available from speciality bookbinding suppliers (see the Resources section page 184).

Book cloth Sized and/or backed cloth, which can be glued without the adhesive seeping through. You can buy book cloth from art and craft suppliers or you can make your own (see page 174).

Bone folder A basic but essential tool for book-making, a bone folder is good for folding, burnishing and even tearing paper. It's similar to a letter opener made of real bone, although plastic ones are also available. Silicone folders are more expensive, but they do not mark the paper so are worth investing in if you become a real bookbinding enthusiast. **(1)**

Steel ruler A steel ruler will not warp so is good for cutting straight lines with a scalpel. A cork back provides grip and keeps the ruler from sliding and damaging your paper. **(2)**

PVA glue Although is it odourless, PVA is toxic, and Health and Safety regulations require workers to wear gloves and masks to work with it, so always use with care. It dries very fast and is not reversible. Some PVAs are heat-set, some are flexible when they dry and some, like Jade PVA, dry rigid and are better for boxes. Wash your brushes very well in cold water after working with PVA. **(3)**

Glue brush Brushes made for use with glue can be found at speciality bookbinding suppliers. Natural bristles are best for working with paste. Cheaper utility brushes work well for PVA.

Pencil Assorted pencils are always useful - keep them sharp for precise measurements.

Scissors Use good, sharp scissors; you may want to get a few different sizes.

Rotary cutter Mainly used by quilters, or people cutting long strips of paper for weaving, a rotary cutter can be useful for cutting down large sheets of paper into the size you need for book pages. **(4)**

Scalpel Sharp blades (plus a good cutting mat) are the secret to accurate cutting. Cork-backed steel rulers and cutting mats help make cutting with a scalpel or Stanley knife, easier. Surgical scalpels stay sharp for longer and are less likely to lose their tips. Olfa knife blades can be snapped off when blunt, which some people may find easier than changing blades. **(5)**

Cutting mat Self-healing cutting mats are useful when using knives or a rotary cutter. You can flatten a warped cutting mat in a photo-mounting press. **(6)**

Binder's awl A binder's awl is a needle on a wood handle, used for punching holes in paper and boards. Etcher's needles and potter's needles can work, too. Avoid the awls with wooden egg-shaped handles, which can sometimes bend and break.

Different awls make different size holes so you may want to get an assortment. Awls are available in student grade and professional grade at bookbinding suppliers. You may also find them at hardware shops, but beware of very thick points. **(7)**

Bookbinding needle Use good, strong needles, as linen thread can sometimes cause weaker needles to break. Some binders prefer to use blunt tapestry needles and punch their holes with an awl. Always make sure that the eye of your needle is big enough for your thread. Curved needles can be helpful for Coptic binding. **(8)**

Linen thread A strong linen thread works best for sewing books. You can dye it yourself or buy thread in different colours. It is also available in different thicknesses. Always wax your thread with beeswax to help prevent tangles. **(9)**

Double-sided tape Photo-safe archival double-sided tape can work well for some bindings. Look out for adhesive roll, too, in speciality bookbinding shops or photography suppliers.

Baking tin When you are just starting out, or working with children, baking tins can be used for paper treatments such as dyeing and marbling, but photo trays may be worth the investment if you use this technique regularly.

Book press This is a heavy cast-iron tool that is used to compress books while they are drying to help prevent them from warping. Book presses can be bought from speciality bookbinding suppliers. **(10)**

Set square Use a set square to make sure your paper and boards are square. The clear triangles with grids (and a metal edge for cutting) work best for accuracy. **(11)**

Brushes Paste brushes can be found in speciality bookbinding stores. Cheap utility brushes can work for use with PVA. Trim them down to 2.5cm (1in) with scissors for the best results. Calligraphy brushes can be found at most art and craft suppliers. **(12)**

Sponge A clean, new cellulose or natural sponge is handy for dampening paper, such as when making paste paper (see page 168). A sponge or foam rubber can also be glued between the cloth and the board to create pillow books (see page 180). **(13)**

FOR SPECIFIC TUTORIALS

Clamp (clip) A clamp is useful for keeping your pages together, such as when binding with stab stitch (see page 150). You can also clamp boards to tables to create right angles. If you are cutting book board by hand, it's best to clamp it on top of a cutting mat onto a work table.

Newspaper You can protect your work table with newspapers or buy clean newsprint so that you do not have to worry about ink offsetting onto your work.

Fabric scraps Any spare pieces of cloth, such as cut-up old clothing, can be used to sew new book covers (see page 174).

Sumi-E liquid ink This Japanese ink is available from art shops and is used to create decorative paper, as in the Suminagashi marbling technique (see page 164). Suminagashi marbling kits often contain several colours of floating ink. **(14)**

Dispersant (such as Photo-Flo) A chemical for use in the paper marbling process. **(15)**

Calligraphy brushes Available in art shops and from calligraphy suppliers, calligraphy brushes have a fine tip. **(16)**

Wheat paste Used for making paste paper (see page 168), wheat paste is available from bookbinding suppliers or you can make your own from unbleached flour and water (1:6 ratio). It can also be made from cornflour (1:12 ratio).

Stamps Assorted rubber stamps are available in many art and stationery shops, and you can even have them custom-made.

Ink pad For use with rubber stamps, ink pads come in a variety of colours, including some metallics.

Sewing machine People do not usually stitch books with sewing machines, but they can work for perforating papers and for making cloth book covers (see page 174). **(17)**

Alum (aluminium sulphate or potassium aluminium sulphate) This is a powder used to aid in pigment retention when naturally plant-dyeing paper (see page 172). **(18)**

Dye plants Chamomile, coreopsis, blackberry, dahlia, eucalyptus and golden marguerite, among others, can be used as dye plants. **(19)**

Gloves Always protect your hands with rubber gloves when treating paper or working with chemicals. Invest in heavy-duty ones or buy disposable gloves.

Rubbing crayons Crayons, such as those used for brass rubbings, may be found at hardware shops, or you can carefully melt odds and ends of children's crayons and mould them in muffin tins for use with frottage (see page 170).

Squeegee This is a wide, wooden-handled rubber blade used to smooth fabric or remove water. It can also be used for silkscreen printing.

Brayer An ink roller, usually made of rubber. **(20)**

INSTANT BOOK

BY ESTHER K SMITH

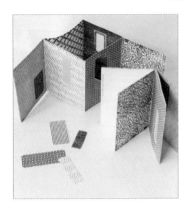

The instant book is sometimes also called an origami book or an eight-page booklet. This six-page, three-spread book, with front and back covers, comes from a single sheet of paper with just a few quick folds and a cut. You can make one with cloth using an iron as your bone folder.

1. Fold the paper in half lengthways, and burnish with the bone folder.

2. Fold the paper in half again, in the other direction, and smooth with the bone folder.

3. Fold the paper in half again, in that same direction, and smooth with the bone folder.

4. Open the folded paper, and reverse the folds so that it looks like a W.

5. Tear or cut the centre fold from the peak to the valley of the W.

6. Bring the sides down together as shown to form the text block.

FOLDED BINDING

YOU WILL NEED
- Paper measuring 21.5 x 28cm (8½ x 11in)
- Bone folder
- Scissors or knife
- Cutting mat (for knife)

Above: Esther K Smith

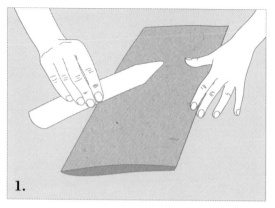

1.

2.

4.

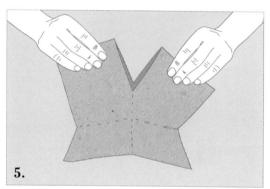

5.

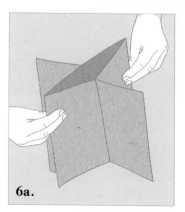

6a.

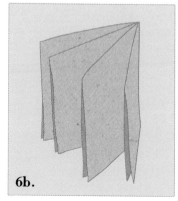

6b.

📌 **TIP**

You can use any paper of any size or texture - heavier paper works best for larger sizes.

ACCORDION BOOK

BY POOJA MAKHIJANI

Making an accordion or concertina book is a great place to start bookbinding. It can be as simple or as advanced as you like, and requires minimal tools and materials.

1. Dilute a small amount of PVA glue with water and apply to the centre of the paper side of your book cloth. Place the book board in the centre of the book cloth and press down. Use the bone folder to smooth out any imperfections on the board.

2. Trim all four corners of the book cloth along the diagonal using the book board as a guide.

3. Apply glue to one edge of the book cloth, fold it over and press it onto the back of the board. Smooth with the bone folder. Repeat on all sides. Tap each corner with the flat of the bone folder to soften the point. Repeat steps 1-3 for the second cover.

4. Fold one of the sheets of paper in half, then fold one edge back in towards the initial fold. Smooth each fold with the bone folder. One half of the paper now has two pages; each will be a quarter the width of the total sheet. Flip the sheet over and repeat. Repeat for the second sheet. You will now have two four-page accordions.

5. To connect the accordion units create a 5cm (2in) 'hinge' using paper. Glue the units to the hinge. You will now have one eight-page accordion.

6. Dilute a small amount of PVA glue with water and carefully glue the first page of the accordion book block to the centre of the back of the hardcover and press down. Use the bone folder to smooth out any imperfections. Repeat for the last page and the second hardcover.

FOLDED BINDING

YOU WILL NEED

- 2 sheets of paper measuring 21 x 56cm (8¼ x 22in)
- 1 sheet of paper for hinge measuring 20 x 5cm (8 x 2in)
- 2 pieces of book board measuring 21.5 x 14.5cm (8½ x 5¾in)
- Paper-backed book cloth (cut to 2 sheets 2.5cm/1in larger than book board all round)
- Bone folder
- Steel ruler
- Scissors
- PVA glue
- Glue brush

Above: Neil J Salkind

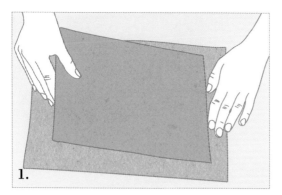

1.

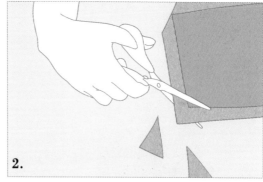

2.

3.

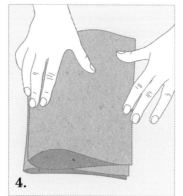

4.

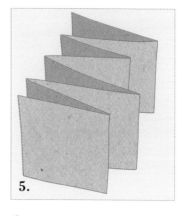

5.

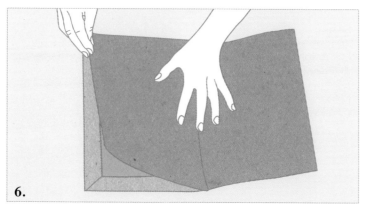

6.

TIP

Using too much glue can saturate and warp the book board and cloth, so use sparingly.

FLAG BOOK

BY ESTHER K SMITH

YOU WILL NEED

- 165gsm paper measuring 21.5 x 35.5cm (8½ x 14in)
- 2 sheets of cover stock measuring 21.5 x 15cm (8½ x 6in), or covered boards
- 9 paper flags, 5 x 10cm (2 x 4in), of 250gsm paper (approximately) or a light card that folds well
- Bone folder
- Glue

Bookbinder Hedi Kyle invented this delightful and accessible book form in the 1970s. Many artists have used it since for books incorporating photos, texts and even abstract paintings.

1. Fold the 21.5 x 35.5cm (8½ x 14in) paper horizontally into eighths, making a narrow accordion or concertina, so that it has eight folds. Smooth with the bone folder.

2. Turn the paper so that it looks like two Ws.

3. Glue three 'flags' to your first mountain fold, alternating sides. Leave a little space between each flag.

4. Repeat step 3 for the other mountain folds ensuring that the flags on each fold line up with the flags on the first one.

5. Glue the outer folds to the book covers.

6. Rest the book under a weight as the glue sets.

Above: Kyle Holland

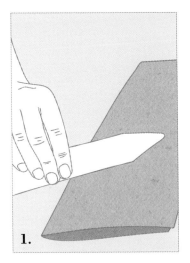

1.

2.

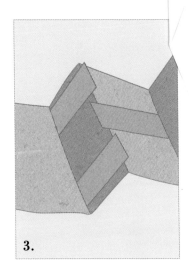

3.

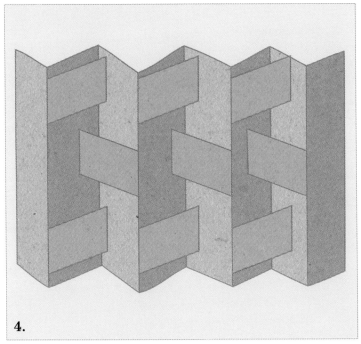

4.

📌 **TIP**

The flags can all go in one direction instead of interweaving with each other. They can be any shape, or even a variety of shapes, as long as they do not interfere with each other as the accordion opens.

DRAGON BOOK

BY WESTERN NEW YORK BOOK ARTS CENTER MEMBERS
RICHARD KEGLER, DIANE BOND, KHRISTA TABAK
AND TERRY WUDENBACHS

The folded book structure known as the snake or dragon book is deceptively simple to master and has a relatively short production time.

FOLDED BINDING

YOU WILL NEED
- 5 sheets of paper measuring 12.5 x 12.5cm (5 x 5in)
- Card measuring 7 x 7cm (2³/₄ x 2³/₄in)
- PVA glue

Above: WNYBAC members; image by Adam Sauerwein Photography

1. Take the first piece of paper and fold it in half. Then open it up, rotate 90 degrees, and fold it in half again. Unfold the paper.

2. Flip the paper over, so it forms a peak on the table in front of you, and take one corner of the paper and bring it to the opposite corner, forming a triangle fold.

3. Hold the paper, with the opening of the triangle facing up. The folds in the paper should make a square in the middle of the triangle and you should place your left thumb in the centre. With your right thumb, push up the bottom of the triangle fold on the right-hand side until it inverts. Do the same on the left.

4. The paper should be split up into four sections by the folds you have made. Two of the sections should be flat and smooth, while the other two should have folds down the centre. Take the sections with folds and bring them together so the smooth sections end up on the outside. This completes the fold. Repeat steps 1-4 on each of the remaining four sheets of paper.

5. Once all sheets of paper have been folded, the pages are fitted and stuck together with glue. To do this, you must hold the pages by one corner and stack them together, alternating open side up with open side down.

6. The pages will slide into one another and are now ready to be glued in place.

7. When you have glued all of the pages together they will fold up compact into a square. You can now glue the covered boards to each end to create covers and complete the book.

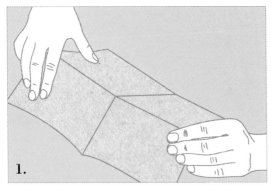

1.

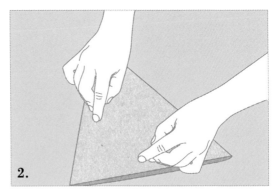

2.

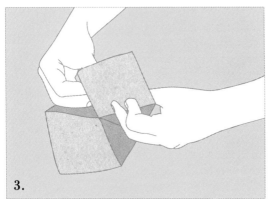

3.

5.

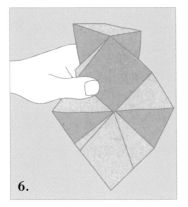

6.

7.

📌 TIP

If you are pre-printing on the pages, experiment with which way you will need to fold the pages in order for them to be readable and consistent. Keep in mind that a portion of each page will be covered by the following page where they are glued.

CAROUSEL BOOK

BY CASSANDRA FERNANDEZ

The carousel binding is a more complex accordion, allowing a book to be viewed like a traditional book or circularly.

FOLDED BINDING

YOU WILL NEED

- Paper measuring 57 x 89cm (22½ x 35in)
- Lightweight wood or cardboard 2mm (½2in) thick for cover
- Strings to close the book (approximately 15cm/6in)
- Parchment paper for hinges
- Coloured paper
- Metal ruler
- Acid-free glue
- Craft knife or scalpel
- Bone folder
- Acid-free double-sided tape
- Cutting mat

Above: Cassandra Fernandez

1. Cut three strips of paper that measure 10 x 72.5cm (4 x 28½in), 10 x 80cm (4 x 31½in) and 10 x 87.5cm (4 x 34½in).

2. With a pencil, mark the first strip 13mm (½in) in from the end (as a margin) and then roughly every 7cm (2¾in) or ten evenly spaced marks, and then 13mm (½in) from the other end for a margin. On the second strip, mark a 13mm (½in) margin, then every 7.5cm (3in), or ten evenly spaced marks, and then 13mm (½in) for a margin. On the third strip, mark a 2.5cm (1in) margin, and then every 8.25cm (3¼in) or ten evenly spaced marks, and then a 2.5cm (1in) margin. Use the bone folder to mark straight lines where the folds will be on each strip of paper.

3. Print a desired image on the first strip, let it dry and then fold the paper along the marks to create your first accordion strip. Fold the second and third strips.

4. Make hinges by sticking double-sided tape to parchment paper. Cut eight strips measuring 5cm (2in) long by 13mm (½in) wide. Fold each piece in half lengthways.

5–6. Each accordion has four folds out and five folds in (not counting the margins). Stick each 'half' of a hinge on the centre back edge of each fold out of the first strip. Then, with the other half of the hinge, stick the second strip 'spooning' with the first strip. Now the two strips of paper are glued with the help of the hinges. Do the same with the second and third strips of paper and the four remaining hinges to create an accordion with three strips of paper joined together.

7. For the cover, cut two pieces of wood or cardboard measuring 9 x 10.5cm (3½ x 4⅛in). Measure down the length on the inside face of each cover to find the halfway point and cut

▶

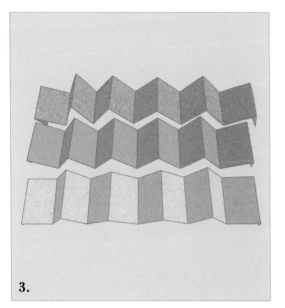

3.

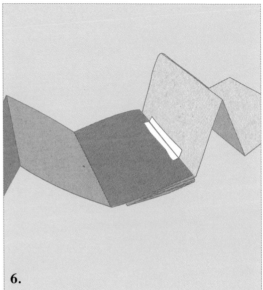

6.

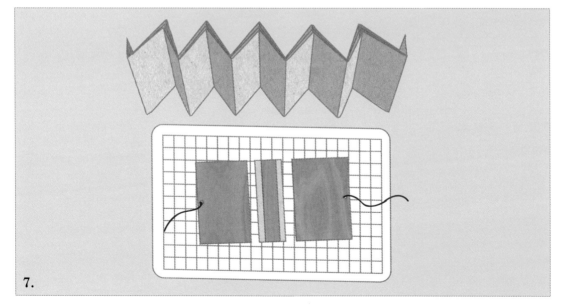

7.

a perpendicular line of about 13mm (½in) long and as wide as the string to be used to close the book. Carve a little groove with a craft knife to embed one end of the string inside the cover. Glue the string inside that groove and let it dry. Do the same on both covers.

8. Make a spine also with wood or cardboard measuring 1.5cm x 10.5cm (⅝ x 4⅛in) and cut a piece of paper measuring 7.5 x 10.5cm (3 x 4⅛in). This paper will work as an outside hinge to hold the spine and the covers together. Centre the spine on the paper and glue it. Leave a 6mm (¼in) gap on each side of the spine and glue the two covers onto the paper. Make sure the strings on the covers are facing in.

9. To cover the inside of the covers and spine, cut three pieces of paper of any colour of your choice, or simply white, with the same measurement as the wood components for each piece. Glue the paper onto the wood or cardboard and let it dry.

10. Back to the accordions: The margins on the ends of the first strip should be glued to the margins of the second strip.

Then the margins of the third strip will be used to stick the book to the covers (see step 12).

11. For the book to be held in place while opening as a carousel, it needs two internal paper hinges measuring about 7.5 x 2cm (3 x ¾in). Fold the hinges into thirds, where the middle third is 4mm (⅙in) to act as a 'spine'

12. Centre the book inside the covers and glue the left margin to the front cover. Then glue the internal paper hinges from step 11. Glue half of one of the paper hinges to the inside outer edge of the front cover; the other half is glued to the inside of the second fold of the book. Close the book and then glue one half of the second paper hinge to the internal fourth fold of the book, and the other half of the hinge to the inside outer edge of the back cover. Finally, glue the left margin to the back cover.

13. Close the book and keep it under weights for a few hours.

14. The book is now finished. It can be opened by tieing the strings together.

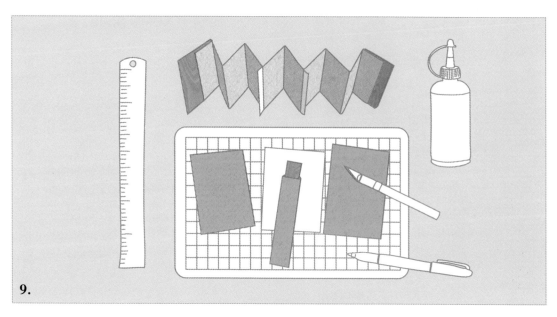

9.

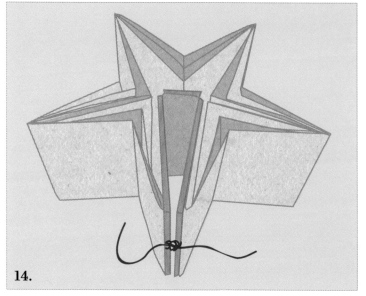

14.

📌 **TIP**
Making a mock-up book before starting on your final one is always a good idea so you can make a note of any corrections along the way.

SECRET MESSAGE BOOK

BY LEAH BUCKAREFF

This secret message fold is another variation of the accordion that forms a compact book.

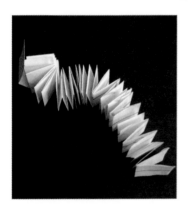

FOLDED BINDING

YOU WILL NEED
- Paper measuring 21.5 x 28cm (8½ x 11in)
- Glue stick
- Scissors
- Bone folder
- Cover paper

1. Write and illustrate a message on one side of a piece of paper - 21.5 x 28cm (8½ x 11in) will work perfectly - and, if you like, cover the reverse side with a pattern or illustration.

2. Fold the paper in half, first lengthways then widthways, at least three times, but keep going until you have the desired page size of your book. The smaller you fold down the paper, the more pages the book will have.

3. Once you've got the desired page size, unfold your paper so that the non-message side is facing up. Starting just below the top-right page/fold, cut the paper along the folds in a spiral all the way to the middle. Be careful not to cut the final page off.

4. Gather the pages together in an accordion style (see page 134).

5. To make the cover, measure the length and width of the pages, then the 'spine', which is how thick the little stack of pages is. Then, on your cover paper, draw a rectangle that is equal to the following measurements: *height = the height of the pages and width = the width of the pages x 2 + the spine width.* Cut this out.

6. Place the cover paper in front of you with the inside facing up. Make a little mark using the bone folder on the top and bottom of the cover where the spine will start and end. Do this by measuring the width of the pages from the left and right edges. Score the paper where the edges of the spine will be and fold the covers in.

7. Using a glue stick (regular white glue is too wet), apply a little glue to the non-message side of the first page and paste it down onto the back cover. Gather the pages inside the covers and your book is now complete.

Above: Leah Buckareff

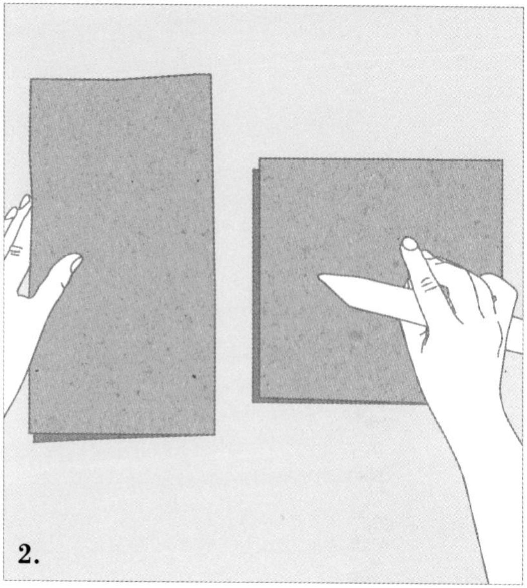

2.

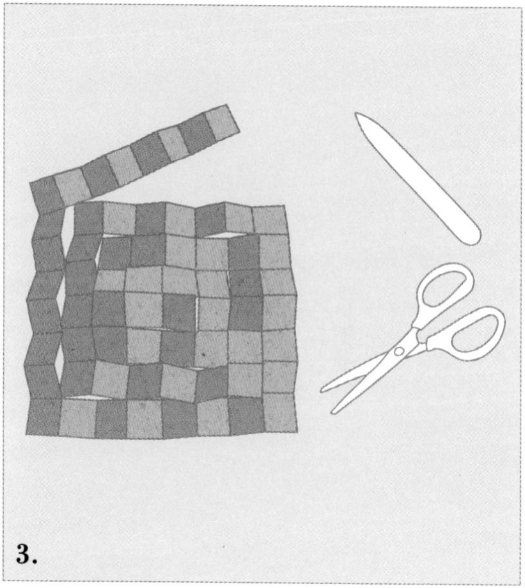

3.

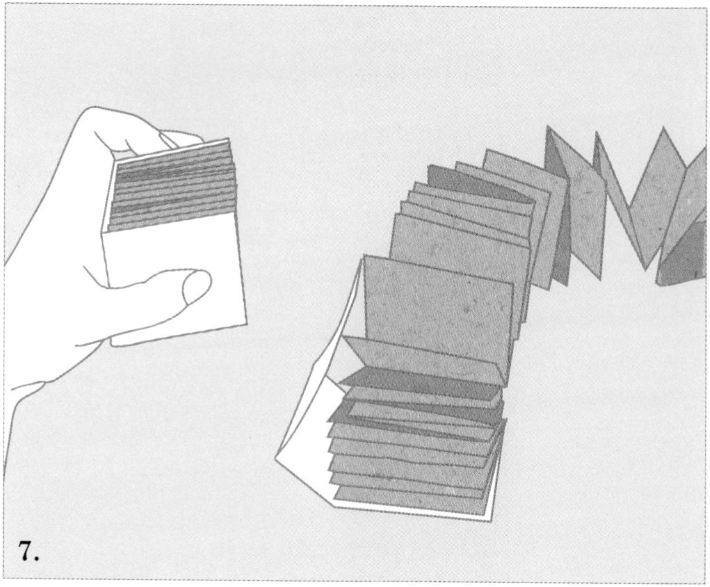

7.

TIP

Using a bone folder ensures you achieve clear, crisp and sharp creases as the pages are folded and then refolded.

PAMPHLET STITCH

BY POOJA MAKHIJANI

SEWN BINDING

YOU WILL NEED

- 5 sheets of plain paper measuring 21.5 x 28cm (8½ x 11in)
- 1 sheet of decorative cover paper measuring 21.5 x 28cm (8½ x 11in)
- Bone folder
- Steel ruler
- Pencil
- Binder's awl
- Scissors
- Bookbinding needle (6cm/2⅜in x 19 gauge, blunt tip)
- French linen thread

The simplest method of binding a single signature codex is with a pamphlet stitch. There are three basic variations of the pamphlet stitch: the three-hole, the four-hole and the five-hole. This tutorial is for the five-hole stitch.

1. Using the bone folder, fold each of the sheets of paper in half to create five folios. Then fold the cover in half too.

2. Nestle the sheets together to create a signature and sit them inside the cover. Then, using the ruler and pencil, mark five sewing stations as follows: station 3 is exactly in the centre of the spine. Stations 2 and 4 are equidistant from the centre (2.5cm/1in from station 3). Stations 1 and 5 are equidistant from stations 2 and 4 (2.5cm/1in from stations 2 and 4, respectively).

3. Using the awl, pierce the sewing stations.

4. Thread the needle but do not tie a knot in the end. Prepare to follow the sewing guide.

5. Begin inside at station 3. Pull the needle through station 3. Pull all but 5cm (2in) of the thread to the outside. Go through station 4 to the inside. Then go through station 5 to the outside. Go through station 4 to the inside. Go through station 2 to the outside. Go through station 1 to the inside. Go through station 2 to the outside. Go though station 3 to the inside.

6. To secure the stitches, tie a square knot around the long stitch that crosses over station 3, and cut the excess thread.

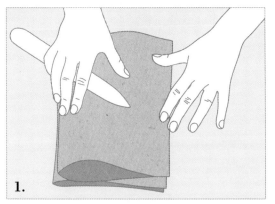

1.

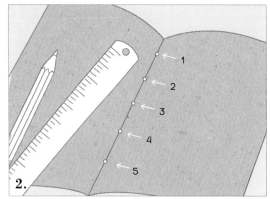

2.

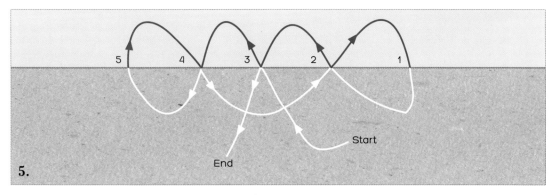

5.

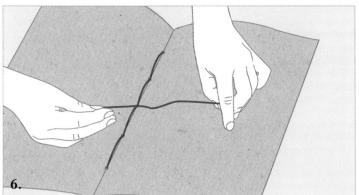

6.

📌 **TIP**

In this technique, the cover and signature are sewn at once. Be sure to lay the signature and cover together properly so the outside edges are level with one another before you pierce the sewing stations.

LONG STITCH

BY ANNA SOKOLOVSKAYA

Although it may look complicated, long stitch is a relatively simple stitch to master. It allows books to lay flat when open and adds a decorative touch to the spine.

SEWN BINDING

YOU WILL NEED

- 9 sheets of any paper (can be the same, mixed, patterned)
- Cover paper
- Cutting mat
- Ruler
- Craft knife (or scissors)
- Pencil or pen
- Awl
- Needle
- Thread

Above: Rima Bueno

1. For this tutorial we will be using three-sheet signatures so you will need to fold each of the nine sheets of paper in half and then nestle them together in groups of three. Carefully cut the signatures so that each of them measures 11 x 13.5cm (4¼ x 5¼in). Mark and pierce the signatures. The height of the signature needs to be divided into five sections. You can either choose to have equal-sized sections or, as in the case of this tutorial, make the top and bottom sections bigger (or smaller). The three middle sections here measure 2.5cm (1in) each, and the top and bottom sections are 3cm (1⅛in) each. Once marked, pierce with an awl.

2. The height of the cover should equal the height of the signatures, in this case 13.5cm (5¼in). The width of the cover will equal the width of the signatures, in this case 11cm (4¼in), times two, plus the depth of the signatures when grouped together (the spine width). To measure the depth, slightly squeeze the signatures together. Cut the cover paper accordingly. You can add about 3mm (⅛in) to the height and width - this way your block will be sitting deeper inside the cover. Finally, you will need to fold your cover and then make horizontal slits on the spine. Use one of the signatures as a guide to mark the back of the spine. Make horizontal slits in line with the awl piercings on the signatures. Be careful not to cross the hinge-folds.

3. Begin with the first signature. Pass the thread through the first station (from the inside) and through the first slit in the cover, leaving a tail inside the signature (you will use this to tighten the stitches). Wrap the thread around the end of the block and

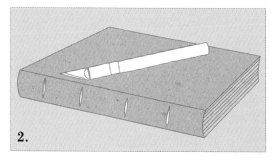

2.

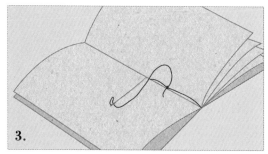

3.

5.

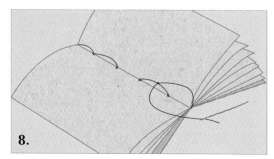

8.

cover, near the hinge-fold, bring it inside the pages and tie two knots. You can then pass the thread through the second station and cover to the outside.

4. Next, pass the thread from outside into the cover and third station, and then from inside out through the fourth station and cover, before finally wrapping the thread around the end of the booklet and the cover.

5. Add in the second signature and pass the thread from outside through the fourth station of the booklet, but not the cover.

6. Wrap the thread around the end of the block, then pass it through the cover slit and into the last (fourth) station.

7. Next pass the thread from inside into the third station and cover slit, then from outside into the second cover slit and station. Pass the thread from the inside out through the first station and cover slit. Wrap the thread around the end of the block.

8. Add in the third signature and insert the needle into the first station of the signature. Do not go through the cover. Similarly to

the first and second signatures, pass the thread in and out; into the second station and slit from inside, from outside into the third slit and the third station, then into the forth station and slit, and then around the end of the block. Once the thread is inside, tighten all the stitches, tie the thread and you are done.

 TIP

With each stitch, ensure you pull the thread through entirely so that each stitch is firm and secure, but be careful not to pull too tight.

JAPANESE STAB STITCH

BY POOJA MAKHIJANI

SEWN BINDING

YOU WILL NEED

- 5 sheets of plain paper measuring 12.5 x 18cm (5 x 7in)
- 2 sheets of decorative cover paper measuring 12.5 x 18cm (5 x 7in)
- Steel ruler
- Pencil
- Binder's awl
- Clamp
- Scissors
- Bookbinding needle (6cm/2³/₈in x 19 gauge, blunt tip)
- French linen thread

There are four basic variations of Japanese stab binding: Kikko Toji (tortoise shell binding), Asa-No-Ha Toji (hemp leaf binding), Koki Toji (noble binding) and Yotsume Toji (four eye binding). This tutorial is for Yotsume Toji, the most common.

1. On the reverse of the cover use a ruler and pencil to mark four sewing stations. The stations should be at least 3mm (¹/₈in) from the spine edge, and station 1 should be at least 13mm (¹/₂in) up from the tail, with station 4 at least 13mm (¹/₂in) from the head. Stations 2 and 3 should be equally spaced between them.

2. Assemble the covers and pages of the book and use a clamp to secure them in place (with the cover still in reverse). Then use the binder's awl to pierce the sewing stations.

3. Turn the cover over so the right side is facing out, thread the needle, tie a knot in the end, and begin binding at station 2 (entering from the back). Pull the thread through until it is snug. Prepare to follow the guide.

4. Wrap the thread around the spine and thread it back through station 2. Then go into station 1 (entering from the front), wrap the needle around the spine, and go back through station 1.

5. Wrap the needle around the head to the front cover and go through station 1 (from the front). Go through station 2 (from the back), go through station 3 (from the front) and go through station 4 (from the back). Wrap the thread around the spine and go back through station 4.

6. Wrap around the tail to the front cover, and go through station 4 (from the front). Go through station 3 (from the back), wrap around the spine, and go back through station 3 (from the back). Go through station 2 and tie a square knot.

Above: Eileen Pandolfo

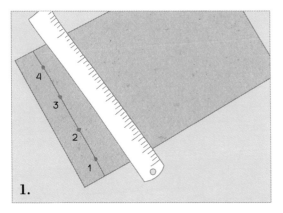

1.

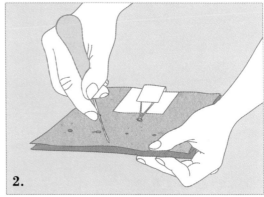

2.

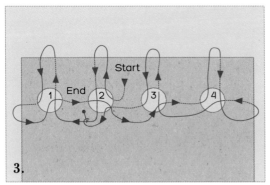

3.

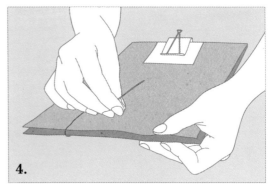

4.

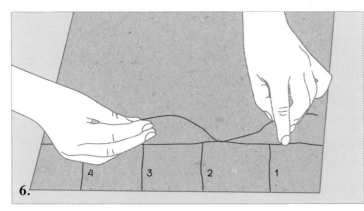

6.

🔖 **TIP**

As the block of this book is created with a simple stack of pages (as opposed to a number of signatures) you can always use different weights, textures and colours of paper for the pages. Just make sure they are cut to the same size.

COPTIC STITCH

BY ANNA SOKOLOVSKAYA

SEWN BINDING

YOU WILL NEED

- 15 sheets of any paper
- Cover paper (plain or decorative)
- Cover board
- Cutting mat
- Ruler
- Craft knife (or scissors)
- Pencil or pen
- Binder's awl
- Needle
- Thread
- PVA glue

The Coptic stitch is a beautiful stitch that will add a decorative element to the spine of a book. It will also allow the book to lie flat when open.

1. For this book we will be using five three-sheet signatures, so you will need to fold each of the 15 sheets of paper in half and then nestle them together in groups of three. You can make this book any size you like, but for the purpose of this tutorial cut your signatures so that each of them measures 11 x 14cm (4¼ x 5½in). Then mark and pierce the signatures. This book will have four stitch columns spaced equally along the spine. This is optional; there doesn't have to be four, and they don't need to be spaced equally. You do, however, have to make sure that each signature is marked and pierced in a position that corresponds with the others, otherwise your notebook will be crooked.

2. Next you will need to prepare the cover boards. First cut two pieces of board to the size of the signatures. Then glue larger pieces of your choice of paper onto the front of these boards, cut the corners and then wrap the paper over the edges of the boards and glue it neatly to the back. Again, using the awl, carefully mark and pierce the boards in line with the pierced signatures. For this tutorial we have left a 13mm (½in) distance from the edge of the boards. This distance is arbitrary; you can make it smaller or bigger.

3. Begin sewing with the first signature. Pass the thread through the first station, from the inside of the signature, leaving a tail (you will use it to tighten and secure the stitches). Then pass the thread through the first station of the board, from the outside - the needle should come out between the board and the signature.

Above: Gina Nagi

▶

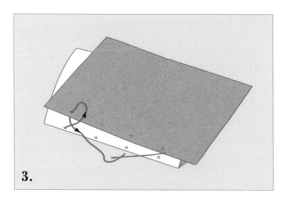

3.

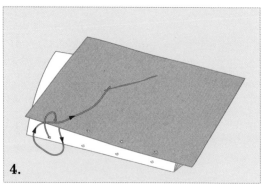

4.

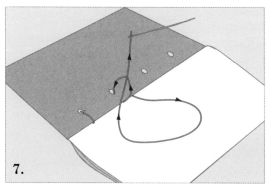

7.

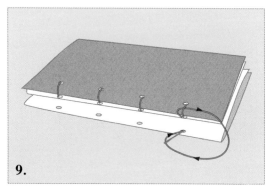

9.

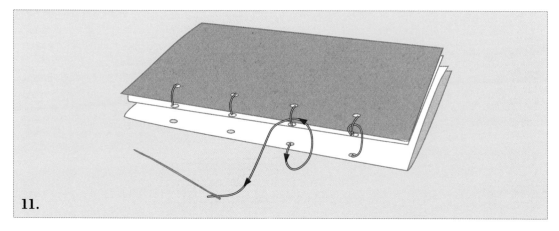

11.

4. Before tightening, pass the needle through the loop. Insert the needle back into the first station of the first signature.

5. Tighten the stitch and knot the tail and the thread together.

6. Insert the needle into the second station of the first signature from inside.

7. Pass the thread into the second station of the board from outside (the needle should come out between the board and the signature). Then pass the needle through the loop.

8. Continue in the same fashion until you reach the last hole of the board.

9. Take the second signature and, after looping the thread around the board and onto itself, insert it into the last station of the second signature.

10. Insert the needle, from inside, into the second to last station of the second signature.

11. On the outside pass the thread from right to left under the stitch connecting the first signature and the board.

12. Insert the needle back into the second to last station of the second signature. Repeat steps 10 and 11, passing from inside into the third station, then passing from right to left under the existing stitch, and then back into the third station.

13. Continue until you reach the last station. After passing the thread from right to left under the stitch, take the third signature and insert the thread into the first station of the third signature.

14. Pass the thread from the inside into the second station of the signature. On the outside, pass the thread from left to right under the stitch. Continue stitching the signatures together. You will be travelling from the first station to the last, up-down, on the odd-numbered signatures, and down-up on the even ones. When travelling up-down, the thread is passed from left to right under the existing stitch. When travelling down-up the thread is passed from right to left under the existing stitch.

15. Now you are ready to attach the last signature and board. This is the trickiest part of the binding. After finishing the last stitch of (in this tutorial) the fourth signature, you will need to attach both the board and the fifth signature.

Instead of going into the first station of the last signature, insert the needle, from outside, into the first station of the board. The needle should then come out between the board and the signature. Pass the thread under the existing stitch, left to right, and insert the needle into the first station of the signature.

16. Pass the thread from the inside into the second station. Pass it under the stitch, between the fourth and third signature, left to right, then loop it around the board. Before inserting the needle back into the second station of the signature, pass it through the loop on the board..

17. Repeat step 16 until the last station is reached, passing the thread from inside into the third station. Pass the thread under the stitch, left to right, then loop it around the stitch on the board and back into the third station.

18. After the last stitch, the thread ends up inside the last signature. Loop the needle under the binding thread, tighten the knot and cut the thread.

12.

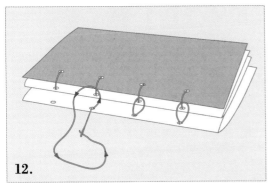

15.

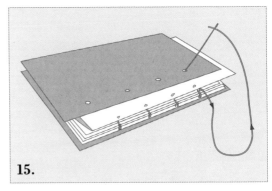

16.

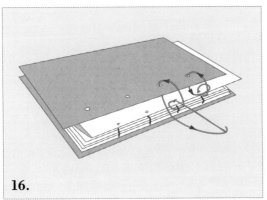

17.

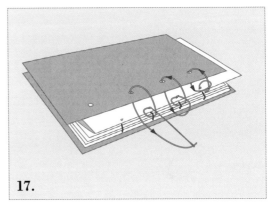

18.

📌 **TIP**

You might find it easier to use a curved tapestry needle instead of the regular straight one. Make sure that you tighten the thread while stitching.

FRENCH LINK STITCH

BY BECCA HIRSBRUNNER

SEWN BINDING

YOU WILL NEED

- 9 signatures (27 sheets of paper)
- Cutting mat
- Ruler
- Craft knife (or scissors)
- Pencil or pen
- Awl
- Needle
- Thread

Above: Becca Hirsbrunner

French link stitch is an exposed spine sewing. It does not incorporate a cover, but once the signatures are sewn together, separate boards can be adhered to the first and last page.

1. Prepare the signatures. This bind looks best with an odd number of signatures. At least three are needed, and from there you can add as many as you like. For this tutorial we will be using three-sheet signatures so you will need to fold each of your 27 sheets of paper in half and then nestle them together in groups of three. This bind works for any dimension/orientation. As a guide, you could cut the signatures so that each of them measures 12.5 x 18cm (5 x 7in), 10 x 15cm (4 x 6in) or 20.5 x 25.5cm (8 x 10in).

2. Measure, mark and pierce the sewing stations on each signature with an awl. To do this, open up each signature and mark a beginning station, then four groups of two stations, and an end station. The stations should be at least 6mm (¼in) from the edge, and at least that far apart. Any closer and you will rip the holes open as you sew.

3. You are now ready to sew the first signature. Thread your needle, then enter at station 1, leaving a tail hanging outside of the signature. Exit 2, enter 3, exit 4, enter 5, exit 6, enter 7, exit 8, enter 9 and exit 10.

4. Attach the second signature. Enter station 10 of the second signature, exit 9, then thread the needle under the loop between stations 8 and 9 on the first signature, with the needle pointing down. Enter 8, exit 7, then pass the needle under the loop between 6 and 7 on the first signature, with the needle pointing down. Enter 6, exit 5, pass the needle under the loop between stations 4 and 5 on the first signature, with the needle pointing down. Enter 4, exit 3, pass the needle under the loop between stations 2 and 3 on the first signature, with the needle pointing down. Enter 2, exit 1.

▶

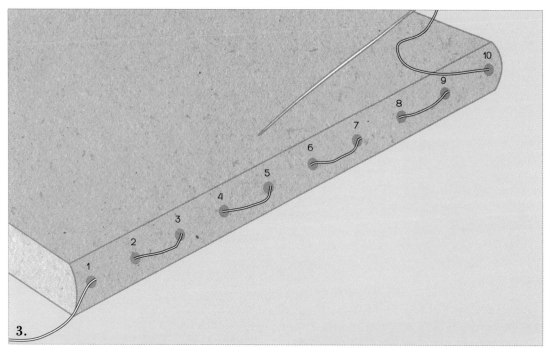

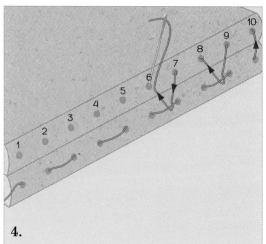

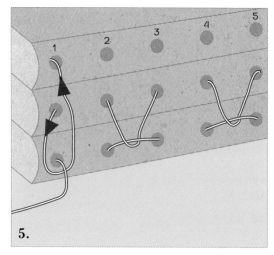

5. Before going any further, you need to deal with the loose tail on the first signature. Wrap the thread from the second signature, station 1, anticlockwise around the tail from the first signature, and enter station 1 on the third signature. Remove the needle and thread it onto the tail left from the first signature, station 1. Enter station 1 and tie off the tail inside. Place the needle back on the working thread.

6. Attach the third signature. Exit 2, pass the needle under the right side of the loop coming from station 3 on the second signature (only the one side, not the whole X created between the first and second signatures), with the needle pointing down. Enter 3, exit 4, pass the needle under the right side of the loop coming from station 5 on the second signature, with the needle pointing down. Enter 5, exit 6, pass the needle under the right side of the loop coming from station 7 on the second signature, with the needle pointing down. Enter 7, exit 8, pass the needle under the right side of the loop coming from station 9 on the second signature, with the needle

pointing down. Enter 9, exit 10, pass the needle through the loop between station 10 on the first and second signatures, with the needle pointing to the left (clockwise).

7. Attach the fourth signature and enter station 10. Exit 9, pass the needle under the left side of the loop coming from station 8 on the third signature, with the needle pointing down. Enter 8, exit 7, pass the needle under the left side of the loop coming from station 6 on the third signature, with the needle pointing down. Enter 6, exit 5, pass the needle under the left side of the loop coming from station 4 on the third signature, with the needle pointing down. Enter 4, exit 3, pass the needle under the left side of the loop coming from station 2 on the third signature, with the needle pointing down. Enter 2, exit 1, pass the needle through the loop between station 1 on the second and third signatures, with the needle pointing right (anticlockwise). Enter 1 of the next signature. Repeat the instructions for the third and fourth signatures (steps 6 and 7) for the remaining signatures, until you reach the last signature.

8. After exiting the last station (whether 1 or 10) in the final signature, thread the needle like normal (if it's station 1, anticlockwise, if it's station 10, clockwise) around the loop below, and enter through the same station. Tie the thread off inside.

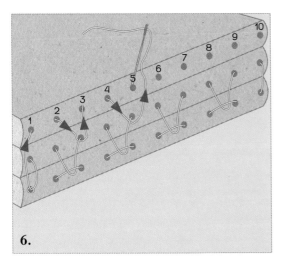

6.

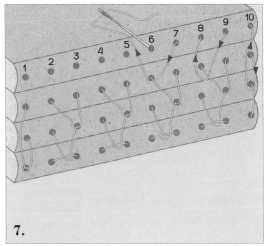

7.

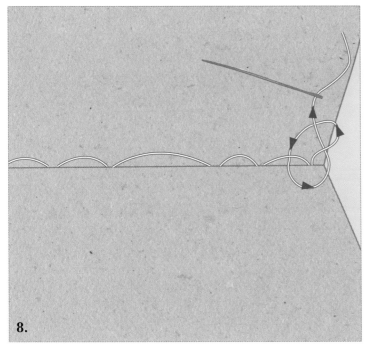

8.

🌸 **TIP**

The amount of thread you need is at least one spine-length per signature (plus extra so you have enough to tie off each end). Always pull the thread tight in the direction you are sewing to avoid tearing the paper.

CASE BINDING

BY JENNIFER BATES

Case binding is a common type of hardcover binding for books. The pages are arranged in signatures and then glued together in a text block. Then the text block is glued to the cover.

SEWN BINDING

YOU WILL NEED

- 40 sheets of paper measuring 21.5 x 28cm (8½ x 11in)
- 2 thick sheets of paper, 21.5 x 28cm (8½ x 11in) approximately
- 1 sheet of paper 12.5 x 20cm (5 x 8in)
- Board for cover
- Book cloth
- Ruler
- Pencil
- Binder's awl
- Needle and thread
- Book press (optional)
- PVA glue
- Glue brush
- Bone folder
- Craft knife (or scissors)
- Cutting mat
- Set square
- Weights

Above: Jennifer Bates

1. Fold each of the 40 sheets of paper in half then nestle them together in groups of four to make the signatures. Place a ruler vertically in the centre of the first signature and, starting in the centre, mark seven stations spaced 2.5cm (1in) apart. Repeat for the other signatures, and then pierce the markings with the awl.

2. Take the first signature, sew into station 1 on the left and weave through the next stations, in and out. When you reach the last station, weave back through to the first. Loop under the thread and tie a knot on the inside. Then pass the needle back through to the outside and gently pull the knot through.

3. Take the next signature and sew from the outside through station 1 on the left, back out through 2 , then underneath the thread between stations 2 and 3 of the first signature.

4. Pass the needle underneath the thread between stations 1 and 2 of the first signature, take it back up into the second station on the second signature. Repeat this method (in steps 3 and 4) through the remaining stations of the second signature. You will be working from left to right.

5. Take the third signature and sew through station 1 on the right (you will now be working from right to left) and out through station 2.

6. This time you are going to take the thread in between the bottom two signatures, loop around the first stitch that joins them, and then take the needle back through station 2 on the third signature.

7. Repeat this method for the remaining stations on this signature, and for the rest of the signatures, always looping

▶

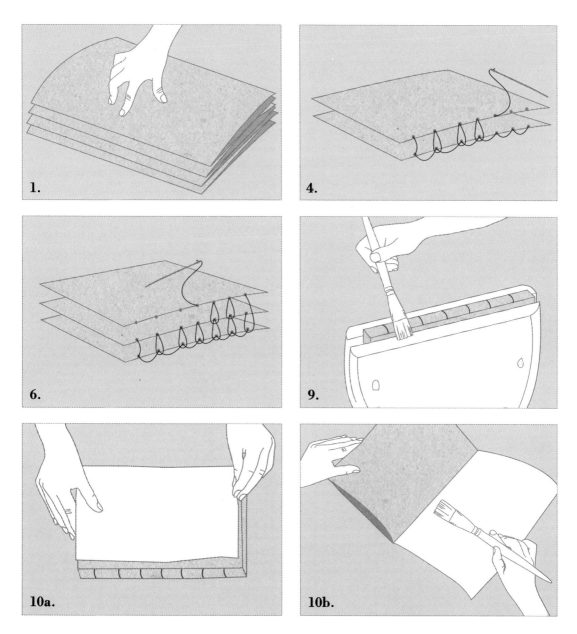

1.

4.

6.

9.

10a.

10b.

under and around the previous stitch directly below. If you get to a point where you run out of thread, tie it off with a knot on the inside, lightly pull the knot to the outside and cut off the excess thread. Thread the needle again, sew into the same station (from the outside) and continue binding in the same way.

8. On the last station, loop under the thread on the inside of the last signature, tie a knot and lightly pull it to the outside of the book, then cut off the excess thread.

9. Making sure the signatures are stacked evenly, place the text block inside a book press. Apply two coats of PVA glue to the spine and leave to dry.

10. Attach the endpapers. To do this, fold the two thick sheets of paper in half, apply a 6mm (¼in) line of glue along the edge of the front side of the text block, and then apply one end page. Repeat on the back of the text block, and then replace it in the press to dry.

11. Once dry, remove from the press. Take the sheet of 12.5 x 20cm (5 x 8in) paper and place it around the spine of the book, using the bone folder to score the folds.

12. Apply glue to the spine and apply the paper, centring it accurately. Glue the sides and smooth them with the bone folder. Place the text block in the book press to dry.

13. Next create a smooth edge to the pages of the book using a blade and ruler. Cut about 6mm (¼in) off, working slowly and evenly through all the pages. You can use sandpaper or a nail file to smooth off any rough or uneven parts.

14. You are now ready to case-bind the text block. Start by measuring the board. Measure the width of the text block and subtract 6mm (¼in) from it, then add 3mm (⅛in).

15. For the height, measure the text block and add 3mm (⅛in) to the top and bottom - 6mm (¼in) total.

16. Mark the measurements out on the board twice for the front and back covers. Then place the spine of the book onto the board, trace down the sides of the spine to get the width, but draw the height in line with the marked front and back covers. Then cut out all the pieces.

17. Take the book cloth (or paper) and lie it face down in front of you. Paste PVA glue on each of the three pieces of board and place them on the book cloth (or paper) one at a time, then smooth any air bubbles out using the bone folder. Leave a gap of 6mm (¼in) plus the thickness of the board between the spine and the front and back covers. Use a ruler or set square to ensure the pieces are glued on straight. Add weights to the cover and allow to dry.

18. Once dry, cut the cover material off so there is at least 2.5cm (1in) around the outside of all the boards.

19. Then cut all the corners at an angle, leaving a small gap at the corner tips.

20. Glue down one flap at a time, pinching the gaps on the tips as you go, and smoothing with the bone folder.

21. Glue the endpapers to the inside cover. Position the text block so that the end pages will have a 3mm (⅛in) border around them. Run the bone folder across each one to ensure it is glued down smoothly.

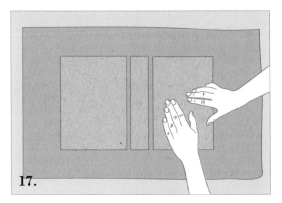

17.

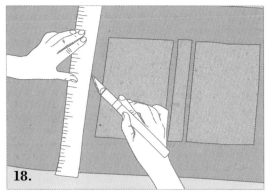

18.

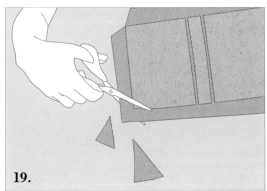

19.

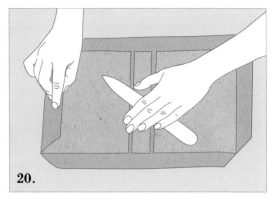

20.

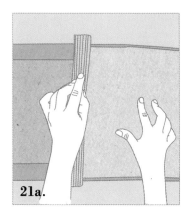

21a.

21b.

TIP

Be sure to use the bone folder to smooth out any creases or air bubbles on the front and back covers and the spine as you glue them to the book cloth or paper.

SUMINAGASHI PAPER MARBLING

BY RUTH BLEAKLEY

PAGE AND COVER TREATMENTS

YOU WILL NEED

- Sumi-E liquid Ink
- Dispersant (such as Photo-Flo)
- Paper (such as Yasutomo's Hosho Sumi Sketch Paper; 30 x 23cm/12 x 9in)
- 2 Sumi-E calligraphy brushes (that match in size)
- Baking tin, 33 x 23cm (13 x 9in) or similar tray to hold water
- 2 small containers for ink and water (small cups like the type used at restaurants to hold sauce work well)
- Strips of newspaper the width of your tray and about 5cm (2in) wide for skimming

Suminagashi, or 'floating ink', originated in Japan and is one of the oldest known paper marbling methods. This technique creates beautiful patterns and textures on paper and is ideal for book covers or inside pages.

1. Lay out newspapers on your work surface to protect it, then prepare the water bath. Fill the baking tin with about 5cm (2in) of room-temperature water and allow it to settle until it is still. The water temperature is not critical, but it should not be too hot or too cold.

2. Prepare the brushes and ink. To prepare the brushes, soak them in water while you get your ink ready - this will soften up the fibres of the brushes. You will need to prepare two small dishes of ink, containing no more than a few teaspoons of liquid per dish. Carefully pour 2 teaspoons of black ink into one of your dishes. In the other dish, add 2 teaspoons of room-temperature water and 2 drops of dispersant - this makes the 'clear ink' that will make spaces between the

black rings. You may need to add more dispersant depending on the brand of ink and dispersant you are using, but it's good to start with less and add more if needed.

3. Prepare the surface of the water for marbling. Take the soaked Sumi-E brushes and carefully squeeze them out with your fingertips, reshaping the brushes into points, and lay them aside. Take a strip of newspaper, and, holding it at each end perpendicular to the baking tin of water, skim the surface of the water to pick up any dust that might have fallen on it. Think of it like taking a squeegee across a window. It's important not to skip the skimming step, or your rings might not form correctly.

Above: Ruth Bleakley

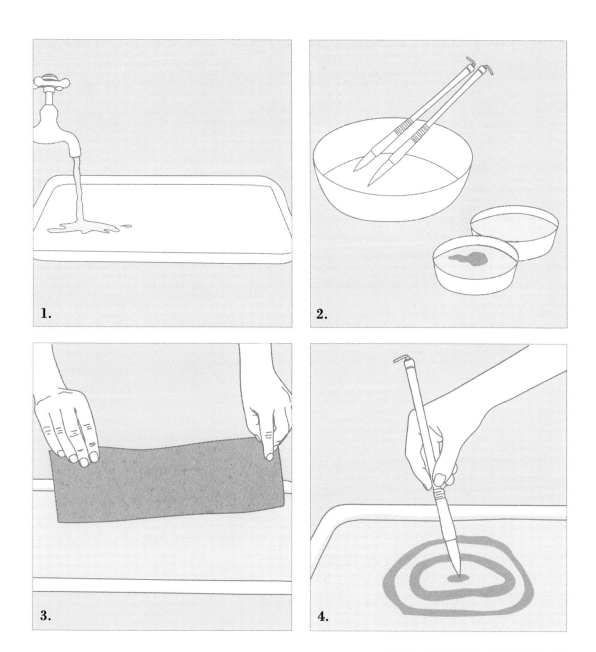

1.

2.

3.

4.

4. Holding one brush in each hand, dip one into the black ink and the other into the 'clear ink'. Carefully scrape off extra ink on the edge of the ink container. With your elbows on the table on either side of your tray, hold each brush straight up (one in your left hand, one in your right hand), with the tips pointing towards the water. Carefully lower the tip of the brush containing black ink to the surface of the water, just barely touching - don't plunge the tip too far below the surface. A ring of black ink will leak from the brush tip onto the water - if it's very faint, don't worry; the rings will start to show up better later. Remove the black brush from the water, then lower the tip of the brush with the 'clear ink' onto the surface of the water, right in the centre of the black circle.

5. Continue dipping the brushes into the water bath, holding each brush in the water for 2-3 seconds, alternating them to form concentric rings. Be patient.

The longer you touch the brush to the water, the thicker the rings will be. Move slowly. Gently push the rings around by blowing on them (gently) or swirling them slowly with a toothpick. The key is slow and gentle motions, so as to preserve the separation of the two colours. If it seems like the black and 'clear inks' are not balanced - for example if it takes you five seconds to make a clear ring and one second to make a black ring of the same size - you can add dispersant to the slower colour to make the speed of expansion the same.

6. Once you have made all your circles (I recommend 50; 25 of each colour) you are ready to 'print' the design on the paper. Holding the paper at opposite ends lengthways, gently lower it directly onto the design in the water, laying it down carefully from one end to the other. Avoid air bubbles between the paper and the design. Work quickly and smoothly - the paper only needs to lie on the surface of the water for 2-3 seconds.

7. As soon as you see the design appear on the paper, pick up the paper by peeling it from one edge. If it looks a little runny, give it a gentle rinse by sliding it under the surface of the water in the marbling tray before taking it out. Be careful as the wet paper is very fragile. Lay the wet sheet of paper down on a clean work surface, or hang it to dry by draping it over a clothes drying rack (don't forget to put extra newspaper on the floor to catch the drips). When the paper is dry, it will be wrinkled, but to flatten it out, simply iron the reverse on a low heat setting with no steam.

8. Print as many sheets as you like, skimming the surface of the water in the marbling tray between each print. Reload the brushes as necessary, but don't saturate the brushes too much or the inks will fall to the bottom of the marbling tray instead of floating on top. If you have too much ink on your brush, carefully squeeze it out until no more drops of ink come out.

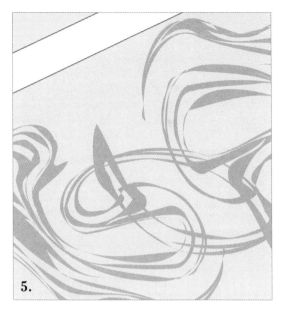

5.

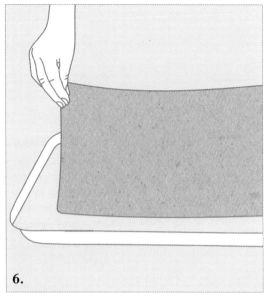

6.

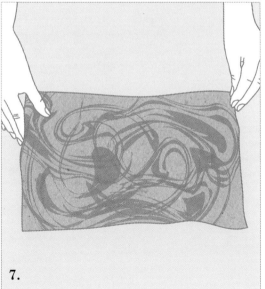

7.

🔖 TIP

If the water in the marbling tray becomes murky, it is because you are dipping the brush too far under the surface of the water, or you have too much black and 'clear' ink on the brush. Start again with fresh water in the tray. If your paper tears, it is because it is too thin - try a thicker paper. If your rings expand too slowly, it may be because of dust on the water surface - make sure to skim it, and if that doesn't work, try adding another drop of dispersant to the ink. If you get mixed black and 'clear' ink, empty out the ink, rinse the brushes and start again. For more troubleshooting tips on the Suminagashi paper marbling technique see: www.ruthbleakley.com/blog/2013/11/suminagashi-marbling-tips.

PASTE PAPERS

BY DIKKO FAUST

A grown-up form of finger painting, traditional bookbinders have decorated endpapers and covers with this technique for centuries.

1. Make the paste by combining six parts cold water and one part unbleached flour in a pan. Cook and stir until it thickens and starts to bubble, then remove it from the heat and keep stirring until it is cool enough to touch. Add a clove as an insect repellent. You can use the paste right away or store it covered in a refrigerator for a few days.

2. Divide the paste into a few smaller containers and add colour to each. You can do this using acrylic paint, tempera or powdered pigments - or even turmeric.

3. Dampen the paper on both sides with water, using a brush or sponge.

4. Apply a thin coat of colour to the paper with the brush or sponge.

5. Comb or stamp the paper to make patterns.

6. Let the paper dry, and then put it under a weight. Repeat steps 1–6 for the endpapers, covers and so on.

PAGE AND COVER TREATMENTS

YOU WILL NEED
- Paper or cover stock
- For the wheat paste: water, unbleached flour and 1 clove
- A substance for colour (see step 2)
- Saucepan
- Brush or sponge
- Assorted items for texturing (such as combs, stamps, forks)
- Weight

Above: Esther K Smith

1.

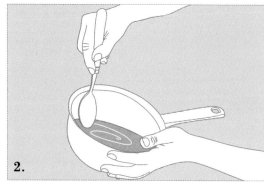

2.

3.

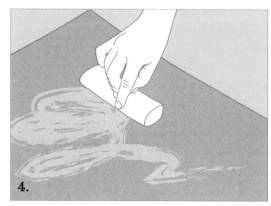

4.

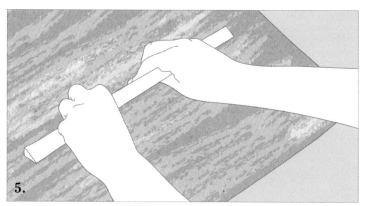

5.

🔖 TIP

You can also make paste from cornflour, baking flour or rice flour, and colour it with acrylic or tempera - any water-based pigment. You can even add metallic powders or glitter.

FROTTAGE

BY DIKKO FAUST

YOU WILL NEED
- Brass-rubbing crayons, lumber crayons or melt crayons
- A textured surface
- Thin, strong paper
- Weights or removable artist's tape

One of the earliest forms of printing, this approach was used to copy documents that were carved in stone in Ancient China. Arist Max Ernst and the Surrealists named this rubbing technique 'frottage'.

1. Find and clean a textured surface. This could be anything, from a textured chopping board to a manhole cover.

2. Tape down the paper, or weigh down the corners.

3. Rub over the paper with a crayon.

4. Use circular, diagonal strokes, and combine colours as desired.

5. You can move the paper to another texture to make more complex patterns.

6. Store the paper flat and use it for covers, endpapers and so on.

Above: Esther K. Smith

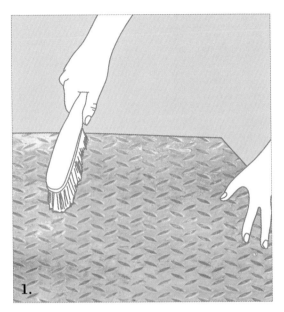

📌 TIP

Instead of using found textures to create frottage patterns, you can make your own textured plates for rubbings.

NATURAL PLANT DYEING

BY NATALIE STOPKA

Many plants and flowers contain natural dye colourants, notably those with the species name *tinctoria* following their genus name. Plants can be used fresh from the garden, or purchased pre-dried and pulverized from a dye supplier. Here are just some options: chamomile, coreopsis, blackberry, dahlia, eucalyptus, golden marguerite, marigold, tansy, yarrow and the leaves of fruit plants.

PAGE AND COVER TREATMENTS

YOU WILL NEED

- Paper (any paper with 50 per cent or greater cotton or linen content, including watercolour and printmaking papers, in a size of your choice)
- Alum (aluminium sulphate or potassium aluminium sulphate)
- Saucepan of boiling water
- Dye plants
- Tray (marbling tray, enamel tray or lipped baking tray large enough to hold the paper flat)
- Latex or washing-up gloves
- Rolling pin
- Sieve
- Lemon juice, white vinegar or ammonia (optional, see tip)

Above: Natalie Stopka

1. Fill the tray with warm water, measuring as you go. Add 1½ teaspoons of alum per litre of water, stirring to dissolve.

2. Next, wearing gloves, take the sheets of paper and submerge them in the water a few at a time. Be careful not to let air bubbles form between them. Let them sit in the water for 20 minutes or until the water has cooled to room temperature. Once you have submerged all the pieces of paper, remove the paper and empty the tray, then rinse and dry the tray.

3. Fill a saucepan with the same quantity of water and bring it to the boil, then pour it into the empty tray. Wearing gloves, scatter a layer of petals, whole blossoms, leaves or pulverized wood in the water, gently crushing any fresh plants

between your hands as you go. Cover this with a sheet of paper, pressing to submerge it.

4. Continue layering plants and paper until the tray is full, ending with plants. For a stronger colour, run a rolling pin over the paper and plants. Allow the dye bath to cool for at least one hour or overnight.

5. Empty the tray, using a sieve to strain out the plant matter. Fill the tray with clear water, and gently swish each sheet of paper through the water to remove any plant material (stubborn bits will easily come off when it is dry). Lay the paper out to dry. When it is still slightly damp, stack it between waste sheets and blotters, and press to dry flat.

1.

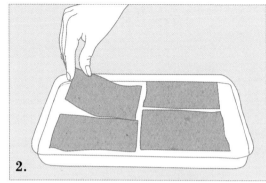

2.

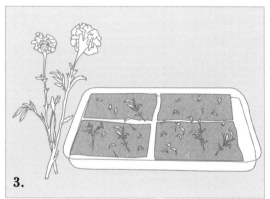

3.

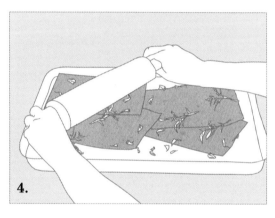

4.

🔖 TIP

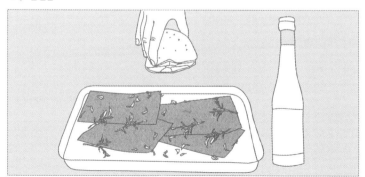

While the dye bath is hot, pour in diluted lemon juice or white vinegar to make the bath more acidic, or use diluted ammonia to make it more alkaline. Changing the pH will alter the dye's colour. It will also shorten the papers' lifespan, but the results may be worth it.

BOOK CLOTH

BY ANDRÉ LEE BASSUET

YOU WILL NEED
- Fabric (cut 2.5cm/1in larger than the project; cotton works best)
- Kozo paper (cut 2.5cm/1in larger than the fabric all around)
- Wheat paste
- Saucepan
- Sieve
- Plastic container
- Spray bottle for water (or bowl of water and wide brush)
- Squeegee
- Window or glass pane
- Brush or brayer

This is a great technique that lets you use fabrics of your choice to create unique book cloths.

1. Make the wheat paste by mixing 120g of baking flour with 240ml of cold water. Boil 960ml of water in a saucepan and then add the flour mixture. Boil at a medium heat, stirring constantly until it becomes glossy and looks like thick gravy. Sieve the mixture if necessary to remove any lumps. Let it cool in a plastic container.

2. Wash and iron the fabric, then cut it to the size needed for your project.

3. Spray water on the Kozo paper and brush it to relax the fibres.

4. Spread the wheat paste straight onto the paper with a brush or a squeegee. Apply it evenly over the entire surface; not too much and not too little - it should be a thin, even layer.

5. Wet the fabric slightly with the spray bottle so that it will stick to the glass and place it face down on the glass pane or against a window. You must work quickly before the fabric falls down if you are using a window pane.

6. Stick the paper onto the fabric. Use the brayer from the centre to the outer edge to flatten out any air bubbles. The outer edges of the paper should stick to the glass.

7. Let it dry. You can then take a blade to cut along the edges of the fabric. The leftover paper strips can be removed from the glass with water and a cloth.

Above: Trinh Mai

3.

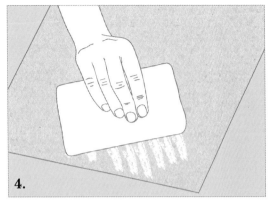

4.

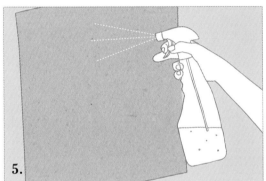

5.

6.

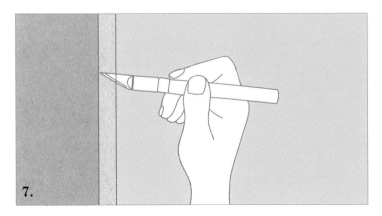

7.

 TIP

Some bookbinders use rice paste or cornflour paste instead of wheat paste.

WOVEN COVER

BY EMMA BONSALL

Woven covers are a great way to add character to a book cover. This tutorial uses old maps, but you could use any decorative, plain or coloured paper that you have. If using maps, select one map that is mostly land and one that is mostly water so as to give a good mix of colours.

PAGE AND COVER TREATMENTS

YOU WILL NEED
- A book ready to cover
- Large sheets of decorative or plain paper
- Cutting mat
- Steel ruler
- Rotary cutter (or scissors)
- Double-sided tape
- PVA glue

1. On the back of the maps, mark up strips that are 13mm (½in) wide and long enough to wrap around the book from top to bottom (vertical pieces) and front to back (horizontal pieces). Allow 2.5cm (1in) at either end. Cut the strips horizontally so that you can read the place names.

2. Lay out the horizontal pieces of the paper in a line and secure them to the surface you are working on, either using tape or by weighing them down.

3. You can now begin to weave the vertical pieces through the horizontal pieces. Start on the left and work your way across.

4. When you have woven enough to cover the front and back of the book, add some tape to the bottom of the woven pieces, leaving enough of the tape to be able to fold over and seal the ends together. Repeat for the top and sides, then fold the tape over to the back. You will now have a woven 'fabric'.

5. Layer double-sided tape on the book you are covering, including the spine, then lay the back of the book on the wrong side of the woven map 'fabric', wrapping it around the book and pressing it down to make sure it sticks.

6. Trim around the edges and then glue the woven 'fabric' to the front cover.

Above: Emma Bonsall

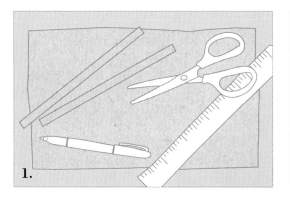

1.

2.

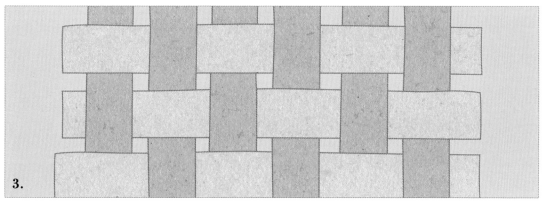

3.

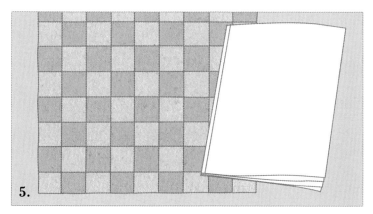

5.

📌 **TIP**

It is a good idea to stack a pile
of books on the completed
covered book to ensure that all
pieces are properly stuck down.

FABRIC COVER

BY MARETH CORDELL

A removable fabric cover only requires a few supplies and is a great way to use up fabric scraps.

EXPERIMENTAL PACKAGING

YOU WILL NEED

- A journal, approx 12.5 x 21cm (5 x 8¼in)
- 3 fabric scraps (see step 1 for sizes)
- Fabric shears or rotary cutter
- Numeric stamps
- Permanent ink pad
- Pencil
- Sewing machine
- Ruler
- Thread
- Embellishments (optional)

Above: Mareth Cordell

1. Determine the order of the fabrics and then cut them into strips as follows: top 11 x 48.5cm (4¼ x 19in), middle 6.5 x 48.5cm (2½ x 19in) and bottom 15cm x 48.5cm (6 x 19in). The middle fabric is where the numbers will be stamped, so choose something light and neutral.

2. Add letters or a Dewey Decimal code to the middle strip using stamps and an ink pad.

3. Place the right sides of the bottom and middle fabrics together and sew along the long side with a 13mm (½in) seam. Next place the right sides of the middle and top fabrics together and sew along the long side with a 13mm (½in) seam. The final piece should measure 27.3 x 48.5cm (10¾ x 19in).

4. Fold the edge of the short side of the fabric about 6mm (¼in) to the wrong side and press. Fold over another 6mm (¼in) and press again. Topstitch in place, close to the folded edge. Repeat on both sides.

5. Place the journal on your fabric, right side up. Fold the short edges of the fabric over the cover of your journal. Draw lines on the folded-over fabric to mark the top and bottom edges of the book. These lines are where you will need to sew in the next step.

6. Once you've marked the four sewing lines (top left, bottom left, top right and bottom right), slowly slide the journal out of the fabric. Press the edges down to keep everything in place and sew the folded sides along the lines. Make a diagonal cut across each corner, making sure not to cut the stitching.

7. Turn your cover right side out and push the corners out. Give the cover a good press. If you want to add any embellishments add them now. Insert the journal; the fit should be snug.

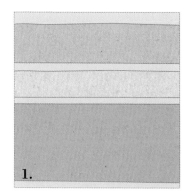

1.

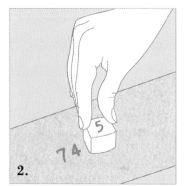

2.

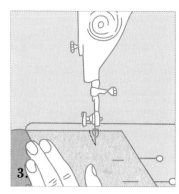

3.

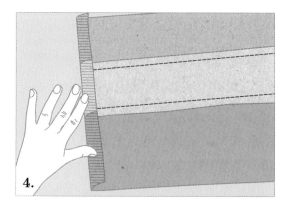

4.

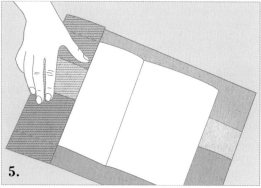

5.

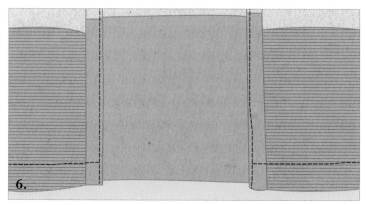

6.

 TIP

When sewing the fabrics together, check the placement of the middle fabric to ensure that the numbers will be facing the right way when the cover is completed.

PILLOW BOOK

BY ANDRÉ LEE BASSUET

YOU WILL NEED

· Book board
· Book cloth
· 13mm (½in) foam
· PVA and methyl celluose glue
  (50:50)
· Glue brush
· Cutting mat
· Craft knife or rotary cutter
· Scissors
· Book press

The pillow book was created by Bassuet as a literal interpretation of a famous eleventh-century Japanese book, where the author, Sei Shōnagon, kept the pages hidden under her pillow.

1. Cut the book board to the size of your text block using a craft knife or a rotary cutter, and then cut the foam with a pair of scissors.

2. Cut the book cloth 2.5cm (1in) bigger than the book board all around, using a craft knife or a rotary cutter. Cut the corners with a pair of scissors.

3. Spread glue onto one side of the board with the glue brush and glue the foam to it.

4. Brush glue onto the wrong side of the book cloth and glue the foam and board to it, foam side down.

5. Press the board and foam firmly down while glueing the edges of the book cloth, long sides first, onto the back of the book board.

6. Pinch the corners of the long sides, again pressing the board and foam down firmly, while glueing the short edges.

7. Leave under a book press until dry.

Above: André Lee Bassuet

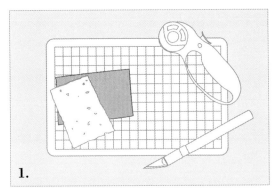

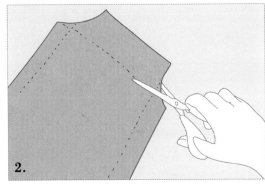

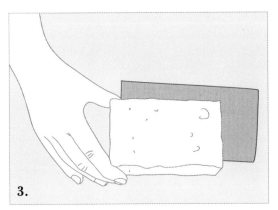

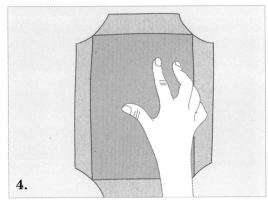

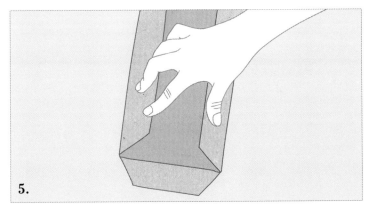

📌 **TIP**

Experiment with different kinds of cloth and see what works best for you.

CONTRIBUTOR DIRECTORY

AG&P Handmade
agphandmade.etsy.com

Alejandro Grima Clemente
www.cargocollective.com/
alejandrogrima

Alice Fox
www.alicefox.co.uk

André Lee Bassuet
www.etsy.com/shop/kowaikuma

Anna Fewster
www.annafewster.co.uk

Anneke De Clerck
somefiddlingonthekitchentable.
blogspot.com

Antonio Rodrigues Jr
AntonioRodriguesJr.com

Anna Sokolovskaya
sas-does.blogspot.co.uk

Askida
www.facebook.com/pages/
Askida/129589630391397

Becca Hirsbrunner
beccamakingfaces.com

Big Boy Press
https://sites.google.com/site/
bigboypressofks/

Boombox Bindery
www.boomboxbindery.com

Boundless Bookbindery
www.larissacox.com

**Canteiro de Alfaces - Livros
Artesanais e Outras Folhas**
www.canteirodealfaces.com.br

Cassandra Fernandez
www.cassa-studio.com

Cathy Durso
www.cathydurso.net

Christer Dahlslett
www.behance.net/dahlslett

Christopher Skinner
www.lestaret.com
christopherskinner.wordpress.
com

Coffee Monkey Press
www.coffeemonkeypress.etsy.
com

Corrupiola
www.corrupiola.com.br

Elizabeth Sheehan
www.sheeprints.com

Emma Bonsall
rubymurraysmusings.blogspot.
co.uk

**Esther K Smith and Dikko Faust
of Purgatory Pie Press**
www.purgatorypiepress.com

Ewelina Rosinska
www.ewerosinska.com

Fatos & Artefatos
fatosartefatos.blogspot.co.uk

Feeding the Lake
www.feedingthelake.com

Flying Fish Press
www.flyingfishpress.com

**Gabriela Irigoyen Handmade
Books**
www.behance.net/gabrielairigoyen

Harrington & Squires
www.harringtonandsquires.co.uk

hellojenuine
www.hellojenuine.com

H&G Handmade
www.flickr.com/photos/
gonnaaway

Hilary Leckridge
www.hilaryleckridge.com

Hinged Strung Stitched
hsspdx.com

Immaginacija
www.immaginacija.com

Inayza
handmadebyinayza.tumblr.com

INK+WIT
www.inkandwit.com

Iris Grimm
grimm-books.com

Jiani Lu
www.lujiani.com

Julia Nitzsche
nitzsches@gmail.com

Karolin Schnoor
karolinschnoor.co.uk

Killside Krafts
killsidekrafts.blogspot.ca

Kyle Holland
www.kyleholland.com

**Leah Buckareff of
Coldsnap Bindery**
www.coldsnapbindery.com

Lime Riot
limeriot.blogspot.com

Little Paper Bird
cargocollective.com/sarahpeel

Lotta Helleberg
www.lottahelleberg.com

Louise Walker
www.behance.net/louise_walker

Lucy May Schofield
www.lucymayschofield.co.uk

Mareth Cordell
limeriot.blogspot.co.uk

Marjolein Coenrady
www.marjoleincoenrady.nl

Natalie Stopka
www.nataliestopka.com

Naughty Dog Press
emilymartin.com

Nightjar Books
amyegerdeen.com

Norman Pointer
www.bardstownbookery.com

Odelae
www.odelae.com

Olive Art
www.oliveartonline.com

Painted Fish Studio
paintedfishstudio.com

Paperiaarre
paperiaarre.blogspot.com

papierdier
www.etsy.com/shop/papierdier

Pooja Makhijani
notabilia.wordpress.com

RAMA
www.ramatailer.com.ar

Ruby Murray
www.rubymurraysmusings.
blogspot.ca

Ruth Bleakley
www.ruthbleakley.com

Red Parrot Press
www.barbaramilman.com

sakurasnow
www.sakurasnow.com

Satsuki Shibuya
www.satsukishibuya.com

Scantron Press
www.dianejacobs.net

Sea Lemon
youtube.com/user/SeaLemonDIY

Serena Olivieri
serenaolivieri.com

Sprouts Press
www.sproutspress.etsy.com

Team Art
www.teamart.ca

Thereza Rowe
www.therezarowe.com

Three Trees Bindery
www.threetreesbindery.com

Twine Bindery
www.etsy.com/shop/
twinebindery

West Cermak
westcermak.etsy.com

**Western New York Book Arts
Center**
www.wnybookarts.org

Windy Weather Bindery
wwbindery.com

RESOURCES

PAPER SUPPLIERS

Adoce
www.adoce.com

Alexander Paper Supplies
www.alexanderpapersupplies.
co.uk

Antalis
www.antalis.co.uk

Cartapura
www.cartapura.de

Daniel Smith
www.danielsmith.com

eco-craft
www.eco-craft.co.uk

Elite Papers
www.elitepapers.com

The Exotic Paper Company
www.elliepoopaper.co.uk

Fine Art Store
www.fineartstore.com

Hiromi Paper
store.hiromipaper.com

The Japanese Shop
www.thejapaneseshop.co.uk

John Purcell Paper
www.johnpurcell.net

JvO Papers
www.jvopapers.com

Neenah Paper
www.neenahpaper.com

New York Central Art
www.nycentralart.com

Paper Arts
www.paperarts.com

Paperchase
www.paperchase.co.uk

Paper Point
shop.paperpoint.com.au

Paper Source
www.paper-source.com

PDA Card & Craft
www.pdacardandcraft.co.uk

PaperWorks
www.paperworks.uk.com

RK Burt
www.rkburt.com

Rossi
rossi1931.com

Shepherd and Falkiners Fine Papers
www.falkiners.com

Vlieger Papier
vliegerpapier.nl

BOOKBINDING SUPPLIES (TOOLS, OTHER ART AND CRAFT SUPPLIES)

A Sprinkle of Imagination
www.asprinkleofimagination.
com

Aboveground Art Supplies
www.abovegroundartsupplies.
com

Affordable Binding Equipment
affordablebindingequipment.
com

Art Van Go
www.artvango.co.uk

Art Journey
www.artjourney.nl

Artisan Leather
www.artisanleather.co.uk

Artist Trading Post
www.artisttradingpost.com

Au Papier Japonais
www.aupapierjaponais.com

Axminster
www.axminster.co.uk

Barna Paper
www.barna-art.com

Bindatex
www.bindatex.co.uk

The Bookbinders Workshop
www.bookbindersworkshop.com

Bookbinding Supplies
www.bookbinding-supplies.co.uk

Broad Canvas
www.broadcanvas.net

Brignell Bookbinders
www.brignellbookbinders.com

Brockman Bookbinders
www.brockmanbookbinders.org

Cass Art
www.cassart.co.uk

Clarkes
www.clarkesonline.co.uk

Colophon Book Arts Supply
www.colophonbookarts.com

Conways Bindery
conwaysofhalifax.co.uk

Damen Papier Royaal
www.papier-royaal.nl

Dasa
www.dasa.com.ar

De Craftorij
www.de-craftorij.nl/webwinkel

Dekora
www.dekora.com.ar

Dharma Trading Company
www.dharmatrading.com

Distribuidora Almagro
www.distribuidoralmagro.com.ar

Fine Cut
www.finecut.co.uk

German Modulor
modulor.de

GMW
www.gmw-shop.de/shop

Great Art
www.greatart.co.uk

Harry Rochat
www.harryrochat.com

Harmatan & Oakridge Leathers
www.harmatan.co.uk

Homecrafts
www.homecrafts.co.uk

In the Clear
www.etsy.com/shop/InTheClear

J Hewit & Sons Ltd
www.hewit.com

Kremer Pigments
kremerpigments.com

Kumetat
www.kumetat-rpk.de

La Dominotería
www.ladominoteria.com

Lawrence Art Supplies
www.lawrence.co.uk

London Graphic Centre
www.londongraphics.co.uk

Maiwa
www.maiwa.com

Nebel Bookbinding Supplies
www.nebel.co.at

Northport Company
www.northportbinding.com

Papertrail Handmade Paper
and Book Arts
www.papertrail.ca

Pen to Paper
www.pentopaperonline.com

Ratchford
www.ratchford.co.uk

Russells
www.russels.com

Shepherds Bookbinding
www.bookbinding.co.uk

TAKEO
www.takeo.co.jp/site/english

Talas
www.talasonline.com

Winsor & Newton
www.winsornewton.com

WAXED LINEN THREAD

Bello Modo
www.bellomodo.com

Bowstock
www.bowstock.co.uk

Empress Mills
www.empressmills.co.uk

Somac Threads
www.somac.co.uk

Spotlight
www.spotlight.com.au

BLOGS, ONLINE COMMUNITIES AND RESOURCES

About The Binding
aboutthebinding.blogspot.com

The Artist Book 3.0
artistbooks.ning.com/profile/askida

Artists Books Online
www.artistsbooksonline.com

Atelier Piano
www.atelierpiano.be

BCF Books
www.bcfbooks.co.uk/index.htm

Behance
be.net

Billie's Craft Room
www.billiescraftroom.wordpress.com

Book Arts
www.bookarts.uwe.ac.uk

Book Arts Forum
www.bookartsforum.com

The Book Art Project
www.bookart.co.uk

The Book Arts Web
www.philobiblon.com

Book Binding
www.bookbinding.com

Book Design Research
bookdesignresearch.blogspot.co.uk

The Book Bindery
www.bookbindery.co.uk

Bookbinding Now Podcast
www.bookbindingnow.com

Cailun
www.cailun.info

Canadian Book Binders and Book Artists Guild
www.cbbag.ca

Carlos Rey
www.aquiseencuaderna.com

Center for Book Arts
www.centerforbookarts.org

Designer Bookbinders
www.designerbookbinders.org.uk

The Etherington Bookbinding Dictionary
cool.conservation-us.org/don/don.htm

Etsy Bookbinding Team
www.bookbindingteam.com

Graphic Exchange
www.mr-cup.com/blog.html

Guild of Bookworkers
www.guildofbookworkers.org

Little Paper Bird
littlepaperbird.blogspot.co.uk

Kuenstler Buecher
www.kuenstlerbuecher.com/mostre.php

London Centre for Book Arts
londonbookarts.tumblr.com

Lou Lou Loves Books
www.loulouovesbooks.com

Mark Tweedie
www.marktweedie.co.uk

My Handbound Books
myhandboundbooks.blogspot.co.uk

Society of Bookbinders
www.societyofbookbinders.com/about/about.html

Stichting Handboekbinden
www.stichting-handboekbinden.nl/site

We Love Your Books
www.weloveyourbooks.com

BOOKS

500 Handmade Books: Inspiring Interpretations of a Timeless Form (500 Series)
Lark Crafts, 2008

Adventures in Bookbinding: Handcrafting Mixed-Media Books
by Jeannine Stein, Quarry Books, 2011

Bookcraft: Techniques for Binding, Folding, and Decorating to Create Books and More by Heather Weston, Quarry Books, 2008

How to Make Books: Fold, Cut & Stitch Your Way to a One-of-a-Kind Book by Esther K Smith, Potter Craft, 2007

Making Handmade Books: 100+ Bindings, Structures & Forms by Alisa Golden, Lark Crafts, 2011

INTERNATIONAL BOOK-MAKING AND CRAFT SHOWS

ABER
www.aber.org.br

Artists Book Prize
www.artistsbookprize.co.uk

The Big Design Market
www.thebigdesignmarket.com

Bristol Artists' Book Event
www.arnolfini.org.uk/whatson/
babe-2013-bristol-artists-book-
event

Brooklyn Flea
www.brooklynflea.com

Cairo Flea Market
www.facebook.com/
CairoFleaMarket

City of Craft
www.cityofcraft.com

CMD (Metropolitan Design Center)
www.cmd.gov.ar

CODEX International Book Fair
www.codexfoundation.org

Fine Press Book Association Fairs
www.fpba.com

Focus on Book Arts
focusonbookarts.org

Frankfurt Book Fair
www.buchmesse.de/en/fbf

Glasgow International Artists Bookfair
www.giab.org.uk

Handmade Detroit
handmadedetroit.com

Hello Handmade
www.hello-handmade.com

LA Art Book Fair
laartbookfair.net

Leeds Artists Book Fair
www.leedsartbookfair.com/2013-
artist-book-fair

Les éditeurs, la foire, France Artist's Book Fair
www.centredeslivresdartistes.
info

London Artists Book Fair (LAB)
www.marcuscampbell.co.uk

Markit
www.markitfedsquare.com.au

Masquelibros
www.masquelibrosferia.com

Minnesota Center for Book Arts Festival
www.mnbookarts.org/theshop/
theshopfestival.html

National Stationery Show
www.nationalstationeryshow.
com

New York Gift Show
www.nynow.com

OCADU Book Arts Fair
apache.ocad.ca/events_calendar/
eventdetail.php?id=3899

Renegade Craft Fair
www.renegadecraft.com

Sheffield International Book Prize
artistsbookprize.co.uk/2013Prize

Small Publishers Fair
smallpublishersfair.co.uk

State of Unique
stateofunique.com

TMDG (Design Festival)
www.trimarchidg.net/tmdg

Tokyo Art Book Fair
zinesmate.org/lang/en/the-
tokyo-art-book-fair

Turn the Page
www.turnthepage.org.uk

GLOSSARY

Accordion An ancient folded book structure from Asia.

Bellyband A strip of paper or cloth that wraps around the 'belly' of a book, sometimes decorative or printed with information, such as the book title.

Blizzard binding A folded binding invented by Hedi Kyle.

Book cloth Cloth that is backed or sized for glueing to board.

Bradel technique A German case-making approach where a strip of paper attaches the spine to the cover boards, also used with split boards.

Buttonhole stitch A bookbinding stitch where signatures are stitched with thread that loops around a slit spine, popularized by Keith Smith in his *Non-Adhesive Binding* book series.

Carousel A book structure formed from several folded accordions of different depths.

Case-bound A bookbinding style where boards are covered with cloth or paper and glued onto a book block or text block.

Caterpillar A dramatic decorative stitch.

Codex A standard book, usually multi-signature.

Concertina A smaller accordion fold, used as a spine or base for sewn or glued pages; another term for accordion.

Coptic binding The oldest codex form: signatures are stitched together in a technique similar to knitting where a loop is picked up by another stitch.

Crown binding Related to Hedi Kyle's blizzard book, interchangeable folios can tuck into this structure.

Doublure A decorative lining used on the inside of a book cover.

Dragon book Another name for Anna Wolf's origami 'snake book', where multiple origami crane bases are adhered together.

Eco printing Also called green printing - an environmentally friendly approach to printing that avoids solvents. Post-consumer recycled papers are typically used. Letterpress from hand-set type can be one of the most ecologically safe forms of printing, since very little paper is wasted and the type is reused again and again for decades, or even centuries. Polymer plates are discarded after use and require one-use negatives. Some print shops even use cooking oil instead of solvents to clean their presses.

Fibre-reactive dyes A cold-water dye, a permanent colourant, which forms a chemical bond with the molecules of the fabric. These dyes work best with cellulose fabrics, such as cotton, linen and rayon, but can also be used with silk.

Flag book A moveable book form invented by Hedi Kyle. It is based on a concertina spine that is similar to a pop-up book when opened.

Folio A sheet of paper folded in half.

French link An unsupported stitch similar to Coptic stitch.

Head and tail The head is the top of a book, the tail is the bottom.

Japanese stab stitch There are four basic variations of the Japanese stab bind: Kikko Toji (tortoise shell binding), Asa-No-Ha Toji (hemp leaf binding), Koki Toji (noble binding) and Yotsume Toji (four eye binding).

Kettle stitch A loop knot stitch.

Letterpress Relief printing from moveable type or photo engravings (copper zinc or polymer plates).

Long stitch A binding style where the signatures are sewn directly to the cover.

Marbling A method of decorating paper. Pigment is floated and swirled in water or a semi-liquid base, and transferred onto paper which has been laid upon it.

Pamphlet stitch There are three basic variations of the pamphlet stitch: the three-hole, the four-hole and the five-hole.

Perfect-bound A misnomer or contradiction in terms, this is a glued binding, as used on a cheap paperback. Perfect-bound books are prone to pages falling out as the spine can get damaged with heavy use.

Portuguese knotted stem-stitch An embroidery stitch that can be used in a variation of long stitch binding.

Saddle stitch A binding that refers to using staples to secure folios to a folded cover. Use stainless steel staples when making books.

Screenprinting Also known as serigraph or silkscreen printing. A thin fabric is pulled tight over a wooden stretcher and an image is applied when dry ink is pushed through with a squeegee.

Secret Belgian binding A misnomer for the criss-cross sewn cover technique, invented by Anne Goy in the mid-1980s in Belgium.

Sewing band Linen tape.

Sewing stations Holes punched into signatures for sewing.

Signature A compilation of two or more loose folios: a folded section.

Single signature codex A pamphlet book.

Text block The groupings of pages that make up a book: a combination of signatures.

Turkish fold A pop-up map fold.

Unryu paper Japanese or Thai decorative paper made from Kozo pulp, with long, swirling fibres. Unryu translates as 'cloud dragon paper' in Japanese.

INDEX

ACKNOWLEDGEMENTS AND CREDITS

Thank you very much to everyone who submitted work and apologies to those whose work I could not include. Special thanks goes to Pooja Makhijani, Western New York Book Arts Center members, Cassandra Fernandez, Leah Buckareff, Anna Sokolovskaya, Becca Hirsbrunner, Jennifer Bates, Ruth Bleakley, Natalie Stopka, Emma Bonsall, Dikko Faust, André Lee Bassuet and Mareth Cordell, who all took time to contribute tutorials to this book.

Huge thanks also to the editorial team at RotoVision including Isheeta Mustafi, Jacqueline Ford, Tamsin Richardson, and designers Lucy Smith and Michelle Rowlandson, for their continued design and editorial support, and to Ellie Wilson for her fantastic project management skills.

Thank you also to Esther K Smith who contributed some tutorials and wrote an inspirational foreword.

As always, this book is dedicated to my Mum, Daniel and Louis.

ESTHER K SMITH

Esther K Smith, author of *How to Make Books*, teaches artists to make books and curates artist books exhibitions. At Purgatory Pie Press in New York City, she makes limited editions and artist books with hand-typographer Dikko Faust and other artists and writers. Their solo exhibitions include the rare book libraries of the Metropolitan Museum and London's Victoria and Albert Museum. Their works are in many public and private collections, including the Tate, the Whitney Museum of American Art and the Museum of Modern Art, where the recent Artists' Alphabets exhibit featured a Purgatory Pie Press wood-type accordion book.

IMAGE CREDITS

All images are copyright their respective copyright holders and are credited to the individual book-makers unless stated otherwise.

page 5 Michelle Skiba of Three Trees Bindery; page 7 Gina Nagi; page 10 Ruth Bleakley; page 32 Lucy May Schofield, photography by Sylvia Waltering; page 38 Ruth Bleakley; page 76 Rima Bueno of AG&P Handmade; page 80 Bill Bachhuber; page 104 Christer Dahlslett; page 122 (below) Matt Fuhr; page 123 Matt Fuhr; page 126 Sarah Peel of Little Paper Bird; page 132 Enclosure Exposure, Elizabeth Duffy with Dikko Faust and Esther K Smith of Purgatory Pie Press, image by Madeleine Boucher; page 168 Dikko Faust; page 170 Elizabeth Sheehan.